Rachel -
you have
such a se...
heart...
contin...
as you...
...through
...chri...
Ble...
Heather
Paul
Ps. 37:4

GOING OUT ON A LIMB

"For where two or three are gathered together
in My name, I am there in the midst of them"
Matthew 18:20 (NKJV)

Written by:
Kimberly Moore and Heather Paul

Unless otherwise indicated, Bible quotations are taken from
The King James Version, and The HOLY BIBLE, NEW
INTERNATIONAL VERSION, Copyright © 1973, 1978,
1984 by International Bible Society, Used by permission
of Zondervan, and The Living Bible, Copyright © 1971 by
Tyndale House Publishers, Wheaton, IL., and The Woman's
Study Bible, New King James Version, Copyright © 1995
by Thomas Nelson, Inc., Nashville, TN.

Front Cover Design and Illustration by:
Valaine Hepner
Website: www.blueowldesigns.net
Email: blueowldesigns@gmail.com

Permission obtained from:
Mary Whelchel
The Christian Working Woman
P.O. Box 1210 Wheaton, IL 60187
1-800-292-1218

Blackaby Ministries International
P.O. Box 1035
Jonesboro, GA 30237
1-770-471-2332

Authors contact email:
goingoutonalimb96@yahoo.com

www.xulonpress.com

Table of Contents

DEDICATION

Heather –

As a child, I would always watch Cinderella and eagerly anticipate the day my prince would come and for us to live "happily ever after." Not only did I anticipate it to happen, I fervently prayed for it. It delights my heart to dedicate this book to my prince charming, my man of God – Jeff and to our three beautiful children, Jonah, Jacob and Emma Rose. The four of you are the answers to my lifelong prayers. Thank you for allowing my cup to runneth over.
Love,

Your wife and mommy

Kimberly-

I dedicate this book to my family for all your love, support and encouragement. A special note goes out for my smart, funny and loving nephew and niece, Brennen and Sierra.

I also dedicate this book to all of my wonderful friends. I love each and every one of you. Without you, some of the stories we include in this book would not have been possible!

With lots of love and gratitude to each of you!

ACKNOWLEDGMENTS

Thanks to……

J eff for reading the rough draft of one of the stories and giving us a two thumbs up when it should've been a two thumbs down.

Bradley and the Waffle House crew for cleaning the waffle irons a day early, so it wouldn't be so noisy when we came in to pull an all-nighter as we finished our book.

Valaine for using your creativity and artistic abilities to share the love of Christ.

Tammy for moving to Australia for the sole purpose of reading our book.

Kathryn for being upset, like any other normal person would be, when you lost your apartment, your office and you car was damaged beyond repair all within less than a week. Otherwise, we wouldn't have come up with the title of the book.

Katie for using the gifts God gave you to add pizzazz and flair to the summary.

Shannon for taking time out of your busy life to read our final, final, final, *final* copy before we submitted it to the publisher.

Paula for your photographic eye that inspired the tree on our cover.

Mama and Momma for writing an encouraging story about each of us.

We want to thank and encourage each and every one of you who in some way contribute to others edification in the Lord through some form of media, whether it is television, radio or literary works. We have experienced and appreciated the wisdom we've gained from Crown Ministries, Mary Whelchel – The Christian Working Woman and Henry Blackaby – Experiencing God, as well as many others. You truly never know how many lives you touch and how many of those lives touch other lives. Your words and your works never fall on deaf ears. If only one person hears what you have to say, who knows how that can forever make an eternal difference and impact on others.

Our acknowledgements would not be complete without special thanks to our families, immediate and extended, as well as our friends, who allowed us to pray for them and put their prayer stories on paper for others to read. Your love and support through the years has helped strengthen our prayer lives.

FOREWORD

"Time spent alone with God is not wasted. It changes us; it changes our surroundings; and every Christian who would live the life that counts, and who would have power for service must take time to pray." M.E. Andross

Do you know people who pray to God with unwavering faith, who trust Him with every detail of their lives, and who seem to have immeasurable peace, regardless of their circumstances? Do you know people who really seem to understand the heart of God and who seek to love and minister to the hearts of others? Do you strive to be one of these people?

Kim Moore and Heather Paul are two such people in my life. They are two women, who I am blessed to call my dear friends, who truly pray ceaselessly. The contentment they enjoy and their motivation for serving others stems from their commitment to prayer. This book is an outpouring of their prayers in hopes that others might learn the importance and the joy of praying too. I cannot imagine two people more qualified to write on the subject of prayer, for they have devoted their lives to it as you will see.

It was no doubt by the grace of God that I was asked to read this book in its initial stages, for it reintroduced me to the power of prayer, by which, at the risk of sounding dramatic, I believe the course of my life was changed. I have always believed in prayer, but I trust that I am not alone when I admit that there have been times in my life that prayer was absolutely crucial, times it was strictly a discipline, and sadly, times it was all but forgotten. It was at one of these latter times that I was asked to read "Going out on a Limb". Why I had let prayer slip out of my life during that period is a bit unclear. Why does anyone? Perhaps because of preoccupation with other things, lack of time, lack of spiritual influence, sin, frustration with unanswered prayers, fear of unwanted answers to prayers, or lack of faith. The potential reasons seem endless…and all too familiar. As I began to read this book, I was reminded that we are called to pray and given suggestions on how to pray. Perhaps more importantly, prayers throughout the text inspired me to quiet my heart and communicate then and there with God. God felt very distant to me at that point in my life, but through these brief prayers, I began to experience His presence again. I was encouraged by the examples of God's provisions and blessings in response to prayer described in Part Two, and I began to pray with more faith and expectation. God moved me to pray more for others, which allowed me to be less critical and more generous and compassionate. I learned to pray for God's will rather than my own and before long it felt as if God's will became indistinguishable from my own. Looking back, I can see the tremendous ways that God changed my heart so that He might work through me. I would not have been receptive to this if I had not been seeking God in prayer. I am thankful to God that he led Kim and Heather to write a book that would inspire me to be faithful in prayer again. I trust that you will be blessed in that same way, for I believe God will challenge, inspire and change you as well if you will pray.

Tammy Alberico

INTRODUCTION

Prayer! What's the big hype? Why are there so many books on Christian book shelves about prayer? Why are there so many sermons preached on it? Not to mention Bible study books. Why write another? How many aspects on prayer can there possibly be? Do these thoughts ever cross your mind as you start to pick up a book about prayer? Do you ever wonder why so many people put such a huge emphasis on prayer? Prayer groups, prayer partners, prayer meetings, prayer chains, prayer walls and the list goes on. Do you ever think, "Prayer, maybe it is a good idea for some people, but it never seems to work in my life?" Are you confused about prayer and wonder how to even get started? Do you long to pray over a matter, sit back and watch Jesus work right before your eyes? Do you look up to those men and women at your church who are considered "prayer warriors?" Do you need a little nudge or push to get you jump-started? If so, my friend, READ ON! The words that lie ahead in this book are God-inspired, spirit-led, prayed over and could be just what you need to get your prayer life where you desire it to be. May this book help lead you in your journey as a man or woman of prayer.

We are so glad you have chosen to partner with us on what we pray and believe will be an incredible, life-changing journey. We desire that the following chapters will better equip you and give you that surge of energy you need to change the world around you. May you believe and trust in God as you seek Him in prayer. Our desire is to teach you through this book the importance of prayer and to show you that scripture tells us that we are called to pray. We would like to reveal to you several tools that can assist you in your prayer walk. We will begin with the basics and then tell you how to progress forward in your prayer life. Our first section describes some of prayer "how to." Our second section goes into more detail surrounding both of our lives, things we have prayed for and answers we have received. We are overjoyed to share with you our answered prayers. Our sincere hope for each of you is that you will be inspired to pray, overcome any fear that you may have regarding prayer and grow vertically in your relationship with your Heavenly Father.

We also hope, and of course pray, that if you have somehow managed to get a copy of this book and you don't even believe in prayer, or for that matter God, that you will keep reading. You have not come across this book by accident. Oh sure, you may *think* you have. You were just sitting there minding your own business, when you randomly started flipping through this book. My friend, it was not by accident that you were in the exact place you were and flipping through this book. It's by a divine appointment that you came into contact with this book. "Divine appointment?" you think incredulously or perhaps even with a smirk. "Yeah right, a 'divine appointment' for me." Yes, by divine appointment with a God who loves you more than you could ever even begin to imagine. "Well I just said I don't believe in God and now these two ladies are talking about a divine appointment - I don't even know what that means." That's okay. There was a point in our very own lives when we didn't know anything about divine appointments either. Whether or not you currently believe in God, we assure you that you have not come across this book by accident. It was meant for you personally.

While writing this book, we have already prayed and will continue to pray for you, our readers. As you read this book, may the following prayer be lifted to our Father on your behalf. May you walk away with a deeper knowledge of and a longing to pray. PRAYER WORKS!

Prayer

Heavenly Father,

Thank You for inspiring me, calling me by name and choosing this book for me to read at this particular time in my life. I know and believe that You have new and exciting things to teach me through it. Open my heart and ears to hear Your word. May I apply unto my life all that You desire for me as I read this book. Transform my life, Oh Lord. Lead me to be a man/woman of prayer. I desire to be a prayer warrior. Thank You, Jesus, for loving me enough to call me to pray.

In Jesus name,
Amen

Mary's story - Lord, why choose me?

Growing up, she had fairy tale dreams just like every other girl. As a little girl she often pondered over her wedding day and how she would live "happily ever after." She dreamed of marrying her prince charming. She dreamed of having children and being a homemaker. She loved her Lord and followed long and hard after Him. She had a sincere heart. She loved people and people loved her. She was real. She was pure, a virgin. She trusted the Lord whom she served.

She was a lot like you, a lot like me, yet, so very different. *She*, was Mary.

What made Mary different? What set her apart from the others? She was a young virgin who was engaged to her prince charming and awaiting her wedding day. Her life was full of sunshine and laughter. She was enjoying life to the fullest and was happy. However, an event occurred that would change her life forever. An angel appeared to her. His name was Gabriel. The same Gabriel who months prior appeared to her cousin's husband Zechariah. Gabriel claimed that Zechariah's wife Elizabeth, though barren at the time, would give birth to a son, John. Their son would set the stage for the one whom Gabriel approached Mary concerning.

The angel went to Mary and said, "....Greetings, you who are highly favored! The Lord is with you" (Luke 1:28, NIV). More than once it is mentioned that Mary was highly favored. Oh, to be highly favored by the Lord! She must have been different from all the rest of the young ladies in order for the Lord to look upon the nation and pick her. So simple, yet so highly acclaimed. *She*, was Mary.

The angel told Mary that she, "will be with child and give birth to a son, and you are to give him the name Jesus. He will be great and will be called the Son of the Most High. The Lord God will give Him the throne of his father David, and He will reign over the house of Jacob forever, His kingdom will never end" (Luke 1:31-33, NIV). He goes on in verses 35-36 to tell her that, "the Holy Spirit will come upon you, and the power of the Most High will overshadow you. So the Holy One to be born will be called the Son of God."

Whew. Were Mary's palms sweaty? Was her heart pounding? Did she feel as if she was on the outside looking in? What were her thoughts? What went through her mind as Gabriel appeared to her? As humble as I imagine she was, I am sure that she thought, "Why me, Lord? Why would you choose me for such a mighty task? Who am I that you would choose me?" We may never know why to its entirety, but we know that the Lord's plans are perfect and He had a perfect reason for choosing Mary.

What a high calling. Not only was Mary chosen to give birth to the Messiah, but she was also the only person to follow Jesus from His birth to His death. He was her son and her Messiah. She gave birth to Him as her son and watched Him die as her Messiah. What a strong woman she must have been. What strength it must have taken to walk with Him through His 33 years, loving Him every day as her very own, yet having to give Him up at such a young age in order for Him to give His life for the sins of the world. What a woman!

We are first introduced to Mary as a young woman who was engaged to be married to a carpenter, Joseph. As we follow her story, we see her as a strong widow willing to give up her son for the sake of the world. Her name is Mary.

The Lord chose her to bear His son. He chose her to walk with His son even unto His death. Why? Because she was extraordinary. She was different. She was set apart from all the rest. He had a plan for her life. He chose her for a mighty task. You weren't chosen to bear the son of God but you were chosen to follow Him. You, too, were set apart for a high calling. He has big plans for your life. He wants to use you for mighty tasks. All He is asking from you is to seek Him, to follow Him, to call upon His name and pray unto Him as your heavenly Father. Her name was Mary, and your name is just as unique. You are set apart. You are different. You were chosen by God for a high calling. Jesus loves you. You are highly acclaimed.

Heather's mom

When Heather was in elementary school, God planted a small seed in her heart. Whenever she could, she would catch the church bus because she desired to go to church. All through her elementary, middle and high school years, the seed continued to grow in her heart, even when she wasn't able to attend church on a regular basis. She moved away to college to become a nurse and the seed continued to grow. As the seed grew, so did her love and thirst to know and learn all she could about God. She has become a beautiful woman of God. She is a woman who puts God first in her life. She puts God in her daily life of being a wife, mother, daughter and friend.

Rosemary

Heather's Story

I sent a message out on Facebook asking for people to give me one word that would most characterize me. Thank you to everyone who replied. I was humbled by all of the responses. The first ten I received are as follows, "amazing, friendly, joyful, optimistic, sunshine, thoughtful, compassionate, angelic, faithful and (last but not least) debonair (thanks Jack!)"

Let me be the first to say that these characteristics are far different from the ones that I would use to describe myself over a decade ago. Yes, I would agree that I am friendly and a thoughtful person; I love people and interacting with them. However, if I had to describe myself, the real me, the me that only I know, it would be quite different. I would say it has taken me a long time to even slightly agree with the above mentioned characteristics. The Lord has brought me a long way. He has "grown me up" quite a bit.

Without going into detail, I must tell you that I have gone through a lot in my life and endured much. The trials and circumstances that I was faced with provoked me to have little or no self esteem at all. I thought nothing of myself nor did I ever think I would amount to much of anything. Along with low self-esteem, I always worried about everything and was afraid of doing the wrong thing. At times that ended up being a good attribute because always being afraid of doing the wrong thing often led me to do the right thing. It kept me out of a lot of trouble and led me to make good choices when faced with peer pressures.

However, I still struggled with low self-esteem and worry. I lived many days in constant fear. It was as if this darkness surrounded me night and day. I was always timid and afraid. Never did I believe I would become a nurse, love my career, have the opportunity to get married and raise a family. Never in a million years would I believe that God would one day call me to write a book and use me to minister to His children. These were all dreams that I never imagined coming true.

Why me Lord? Who am I that you would use me? I have not the answer to that question and will always wonder the answer, but I rest assured that He knows the answer and thus here I am. I am an open vessel ready for God to use. Time and time again I have prayed, "Lord, if You can use anyone You can use me. I come before You tired, weary, doubtful and full of fear." I came to Him that way and He changed me, turned me around and molded me. Job 10:9, NIV, states, "Remember that you molded me like clay..." He is still molding me into a woman of God that He can use.

Though I struggled with fear, worry and low self-esteem, I rested in the fact that I had the freedom to pray and when I would pray, all of my troubles for that moment would fade away. Prayer was like a safe haven for me. When I prayed, it was as if the world stood still and was filled with only the Lord and I. The two of us and no one else. I was safe. I gave my worries to God. When I prayed, I didn't have low self-esteem, because in His eyes I was beautiful. He made me and loved me. Psalm 139:14a (NIV), says that "....I am fearfully and wonderfully made." How refreshing is prayer! Oh, to God be the glory for allowing us to pray. How magnificent is He that He would want to commune with a sinner such as me. He loved me enough to call me to live a life of being sold out to prayer. He has brought me a long way from the meek, timid person that I used to be. He has transformed my life. 2 Timothy 1:7, KJV, tells me that, "God hath not given us a spirit of fear (timidity); but of power, and of love, and of a sound mind." Why would the Lord use me? The same reason that He desires to use you. We are His people. He has called and raised us up to be His children. Children that He desires to use in extraordinary ways. All we have to do is be able and willing.

Moses' story – Lord I don't speak eloquently

Let's take a look at Moses' childhood and his life. Moses was born to a Levite woman. His mother put him in a papyrus basket and set him sailing on the Nile. His mother wanted to spare his life as Pharaoh had sent out an order not to let any newborn males live. Interestingly enough, Moses' was found in the Nile River by Pharaoh's daughter. She kept him and raised him as her own. He went from being a Hebrew to an Egyptian prince just like that!

Not only did this amazing thing happen in his early life, but down the road, God would call him by name and desire to use him. God desired for Moses to be the chosen one to bring the Israelites out of Egypt. Wow! What a job. Moses must have been a very confident person and believed that he should have been chosen, right? He knew he would be a great leader and had no doubts about it, right? Wrong! Refer to Exodus 3 and read just how scared Moses was and how unsure he was that God had the right guy. Exodus 3:11-13, NIV explains the conversation between Moses and God as they went back and forth over why Moses was chosen for the job. "Moses said to the Lord, "O Lord, I have never been eloquent, neither in the past nor since you have spoken to your servant. I am slow of speech and tongue." The Lord said to him, "Who gave man his mouth? Who makes him deaf or mute? Who gives him sight or makes him blind? Is it not I, the Lord? Now go; I will help you speak and will teach you what to say." But Moses said, "O Lord, please send someone else to do it." Moses would have never volunteered himself for the great task that the Lord called him to do. He was insecure and his speech was not very eloquent. He didn't have the confidence in himself, but God sure did. God knew that Moses would never be alone for He planned to be with him every step of the way.

Do you ever feel like Moses felt when God called him for such a great task? As the Lord has called us to write a book, we too felt inadequate to do such a task for the Lord. Why would He, the creator of the heavens and earth, call us for such a job? Why would the same God who set the stars in place, call us to a lifetime of prayer?

We are only ordinary people just like each of you reading this book. Why is God calling you to the very thing that He has called you to? Regardless of the person or situation, the underlying purpose is the same, to draw people to Himself. Not only does He desire to draw people to Himself but He chooses ordinary people like us to get His message across. As you read this book, please know that much prayer has been put into it's every process and we pray that every single word is inspired by the Lord. May the Lord use our desire and call to prayer in order to transform your life and draw you closer to Him simply by communicating with Him through prayer.

Kim's Mom

Kim was only five years old when she came to me to ask questions about how to "let Jesus in my heart <u>forever</u>." This was the question that I had prayed about since the day she was born. As we talked, her face lit up and she told me she "was ready to give her heart to Jesus."

I asked her on that Sunday if she wanted me to walk down the aisle at the end of the service with her. She replied, "No thank you momma. Jesus is going with me." When the song, "Have Thine Own Way, Lord" began, Kim looked up at me and said, "Momma, I'm going."

She walked quickly and quietly down the aisle with the sweetest smile on her face. Such joy filled two parents' hearts as she told our pastor she wanted Jesus to come into her heart and live. The pastor stopped the music and told the congregation what Kim had told him.

Then, there was movement at the back of the church, as an older man started up the aisle. When he reached the pastor, he told him that he had been coming to church off and on for about 60 years but never had the courage "to come down that long aisle, until that little girl walked so courageously down the aisle herself." "I feel good now," he told the pastor. After we got home, Kim looked at us and said, "I don't think I gave that man courage. I think Jesus did it."

Mark 9:36-37 (TLB): "Then he placed a little child among them; and taking the child in his arms he said to them, 'Anyone who welcomes a little child like this in my name is welcoming me, and anyone who welcomes me is welcoming my Father who sent me!"

Matthew 19:14-15 (TLB): "But Jesus said, 'Let the little children come to me, and don't prevent them. For such is the Kingdom of Heaven.' And he put his hands on their heads and blessed them before he left."

Janis

Kim's Story

Who am I to think God would use me? I'm not worthy. I'm not good enough. How often have these thoughts gone through your head? Probably as often as they have mine. I can relate to how Moses' must have felt when God called him to do things for Him.

Let's start with who I was growing up. I was shy. Really shy. Extremely shy. Okay, to be perfectly honest, painfully shy. When I was ten years old and in the fourth grade, I was not only shy but I also considered myself a "nerd." Yep, that was me alright. I wore huge, thick, big-rimmed glasses. (Of course it was the eighties and those *were* actually in style then.) In addition to being the brain in the class, I was also bean pole skinny. Academics came really easy to me. So easy in fact that sometimes I was reluctant to admit how fast I learned new facts. But when you are ten years old, being "smart" is not "cool." Having a love and passion for science and math is not exactly popular. Add in some self-consciousness, insecurity and a whole lot of fear of meeting new people and that was me.

I was so quiet in the fourth grade, that I can only remember talking to a small handful of classmates for the whole year. Can you imagine? Maybe you can, if that's you. I remember there were several people in the class that I didn't talk to at all for the entire year. It was painful to just wait for someone to come up and talk to me. I was so quiet, that I was voted by my classmates as "Quietest" and "Shyest." I was actually given ribbons to take home with me that labeled me as such at the end of the year, as if it was an honor!

I already criticized myself. I thought things like, "I shouldn't be so quiet" and "I need to be more talkative." But the more I criticized myself, the harder I made it on myself, the more pressure I felt and then I would certainly be too stressed out to talk to anyone!

And heaven forbid that I would have to do *anything* that required me to talk in front of the class! Please, oh please, don't make me stand up there in front of everyone. Please don't put me in the spotlight!

Then one day after years of being quiet and shy, God spoke to me through His word. It was so tender and touching. Genesis 1:27, NKJV, "So God created man in His own image; in the image of God He created him; male and female He created them." God created ME! God did that. He made me and He made me "in HIS own image!" He made me the way I am for a reason and a purpose. The Almighty God of the universe made me *in His image*. I came to the realization that when I criticized myself for being quiet, I was also criticizing the very attributes that God had given me. Furthermore, being quiet must also be an attribute of God because after all I'm created, "in His image." So if I criticize myself for being quiet, then am I not also criticizing God for being quiet? From that moment on, I stopped criticizing myself, because I realized I was criticizing God's creation.

We are all part of the body of believers and each of us plays a different role. Paul tells us in 1 Corinthians 12:27, TLB, "...all of you together are the one body of Christ, and each one of you is a separate and necessary part of it." Paul goes on to describe different roles that each one of us is gifted at. We do not all have the exact same talents or roles in life. Otherwise, I think things could get pretty boring, pretty quickly. However, each of us is necessary!

The ultimate purpose above all else is to glorify God. He made me to bring Him glory. What once was painful to me is now a privilege and an honor. I am the listener. I am the one people seek out when they truly need their problems heard. Now, if and when I am quiet, it is not regarded by me as a negative attribute. I know that fear used to be at the center of my quietness. Faith and courage now stand in the center.

So let's fast forward to the present. I've come a long, long way since the fourth grade. God has done some amazing things in my life. I've gone from being too timid to even make eye contact with people or raise my hand in class to living on my own in another country. I've had many adventures and embraced meeting new people along the way.

I have since run across several people from my life, who have been astounded by what I did. They have made remarks such as, "I can't believe YOU did that! I remember how quiet you used to be and *you* moved to another country!?!" I say these things to offer encouragement to you. My friend, I do not know your personality, your background or what your current life situation is. However, if the Almighty Creator of the universe can take a timid, meek, extremely shy, little girl and turn her around into a brave, bold woman of faith, as He did for me then He can do the same for you. No matter what is going on with you or where you are, God can do miraculous things in you and through you.

God can and will use anyone. You don't have to be perfect to come to God. You don't have to get yourself together and in order. That's His job. He just says to come.

PART I

PRAYER 101

Pumping Iron

How many informercials have your viewed in your life-time? What about the ones selling exercise equipment? You do not have to admit the answer to this next question out loud (unless the Spirit leads you to, of course) but how many different exercise equipment pieces, home workout videos, etc. do you actually own? You know the old joke, "I bought a treadmill in order to use it to get physically fit and now the only thing that it is used for is to hang my clothes on." You may chuckle, but isn't there some truth to this statement? You may not have a treadmill in your home, but we imagine that more of you than not have at least one piece of exercise equipment or an exercise video in your home that could now be classified as a "dust collector."

To get to the point we are trying to make, we must ask you some questions. Why did you make that purchase? What sold you on that item? How long did the 'gimmick' work? Why are you no longer using that idea to get physically fit? And, why did you move on to some other idea for physical fitness/weight loss? Even if it was for just one week or so, you were once sold on that item. You believed in that item, you had faith in it and you just knew that it was going to transform your life and your self image. But did it? The only thing it is changing now is the amount of dust that is not able to accumulate on other items.

Just as the infomercial's goal was to "sell" you the advertised item, we too, desire to introduce you to a life changing idea called prayer! Prayer is not a gimmick. Prayer is not something that we are trying to "sell" you on for you to participate in just for the time being. First and foremost, our desire is that you will get on board and allow God to do amazing things in and through your life as a result of prayer.

Prayer works! We honestly believe that! Prayer is our passion. We are behind prayer 100% and know that the Lord is behind you, calling you to a deeper walk, a deeper longing for and a deeper desire to pray. He has so much to reveal to you if only you would come alongside Him in the awesome journey of prayer.

There is no other way for you to develop your prayer life than by praying. No one else can do it for you. You are the only one who can make yourself do it. You have a conscious decision to make. That decision is whether or not you are going to pray. Hebrews 12:1, NKJV, "...run with endurance the race that is set before us." So get out there and pray! In Ecclesiastes 11:4, TLB, it states, "If you wait for the perfect conditions, you will never get anything done."

We want you to gain a little understanding of who, what, when, where and why of prayer. Then we want to go over the "how to" of prayer. These next chapters reveal to you tools to assist you as you develop and strengthen your prayer life. We discuss using a prayer box, journaling, memorizing scripture and other books to help assist you in your own personal journey of prayer.

CHAPTER ONE

GETTING STARTED

Who

Who are you praying to? God. He is our Lord, our Savior and our Heavenly Father. He is our provider, protector and creator. He is Jesus! "God so loved the world that He gave His one and only son, that whoever believes in Him shall not perish but have eternal life" (John 3:16, NIV).

Have you heard of the trinity? The Father, Son and Holy Spirit all make up the trinity. Let's look at water to better understand the concept. The molecular structure of water is still H2O whether it is ice, liquid or vapor. There is a certain temperature and pressure at which all three can co-exist. Yet each one serves a different purpose. In the same way, the Father, Son and Holy Spirit are all God; the God to whom we pray. There is God the Father, Jesus the Son and the Holy Spirit who leads and guides us. In John 14:26, NIV, Jesus said, "But the Counselor, the Holy Spirit, whom the Father will send in My name, will teach you all things and will remind you of everything I have said to you."

As previously mentioned, God gave His Son in order for us to have eternal life. He loves you that much! The only way to God is through His Son. "As many as received Him, to them He gave the right to become children of God, even to those who believe in His name" (John 1:12, NIV). We are sinful from birth and have spiritual separation from God. "For all have sinned and fall short of the glory of God" (Romans 3:23, NIV). Through Jesus alone we are able to be united with God. "The wages of sin is death, but the gift of God is eternal life in Christ Jesus our Lord" (Romans 6:23, NIV). We must receive Christ through faith as our Savior and Lord. "By grace you have been saved through faith; and that not of yourselves, it is the gift of God; not as a result of works that no one should boast" (Ephesians 2: 8-9, NIV). We can not earn salvation, it is a free gift from God. God is calling each of us unto himself. "Behold, I stand at the door and knock; if any one hears My voice and opens the door, I will come in to him" (Revelation 3:20, NIV).

If you have never come to the point in your life where you made a decision to accept Christ as your personal Lord and Savior, we invite you to pray the following prayer.

Father God,

I come to You a sinner. I believe in You and I need You. Thank You sending Your Son to die on the cross for my sins and allowing me to accept Him as my Savior. Thank You for forgiving me of my sins and giving me eternal life. I give You my life. I place You in control. Mold me into the man/woman that You desire for me to be.

In Jesus name,
Amen

What

After having read "who" we are praying to, you may wonder "what" to pray. Let's first start with the most popular modeled prayer. You may have heard it before or you may have heard it being referred to. It is the Lord's Prayer. Matthew 6:9-13, KJV, states to pray along these lines,

> *"Our Father which are in heaven, Hallowed be thy name. Thy kingdom come, thy will be done on earth, as it is in heaven. Give us this day our daily bread. And forgive us our debts, as we forgive our debtors. And lead us not into temptation, but deliver us from evil: For thine is the kingdom, and the power, and the glory, forever. Amen."*

Come humbly before Him and speak to Him for He is listening. He knows our hearts. The Lord's Prayer is the prayer of all prayers for it is exactly the words Jesus Himself recited. Jesus starts out with reverence to God. Then He asks for His Father's will to be done. From there He goes on to ask for the Lord's provision, forgiveness and protection in His life. What better prayer could there possibly be to model? It is very simple and straight from the heart yet full of passion and desire. Come to Him with your requests as well as praises with passion and desire, for Jesus has already gone before you with the ultimate prayer and has prayed it on your behalf. Come willingly and with a pure heart.

The Lord calls us to come as we are. We don't have to be fancy and use big words. Matthew 6:7-8 TLB states, "Don't recite the same prayer over and over as the heathen do, who think prayers are answered only by repeating them again and again." Remember, your Father knows exactly what you need even before you ask Him. The focus of prayer is not only what we pray, but also the condition of our heart when we pray.

When

When to pray is best decided on an individual basis. You can pray morning, noon or night. You be the judge. You decide when the best time is for *you* to pray. We really don't think it matters to the Lord. He is up and ready to hear from you 24/7. All that matters is that you give God your best.

For some of you, it may be best to come to God early in the morning before the craziness of the day gets started. Give Him your day before your day begins, when you are well rested and can come to Him in the quiet of the morning. It's not always easy to get up early. Okay, okay, so maybe for some of you morning people out there, it's exciting to get up early for any reason, but it takes discipline to get up early. However, Hebrews 12:11 from the NIV version tells us that, "no discipline seems pleasant at the time, but painful. Later on, however, it produces a harvest of righteousness and peace for those who have been trained by it." Mark 1:35, NIV, also tells us that, "very early in the morning, while it was still dark, Jesus got up, left the house and went off to a solitary place, where He prayed." Talk about early. The Bible tells us that it was still dark. To me, that is God's inspiring way of telling us that the rooster had not even crowed. Had there been a Starbuck's in Jesus' time, it wouldn't have been open that early. Jesus got up before the rooster crowed and without coffee in order to pray. Now that is dedication.

The following analogy is one regarding prayer at the beginning of the day. Imagine the Lord was coming to your home for dinner. Would you make Him wait outside on the front porch while you are busy cleaning up the inside of the house? Would you make Him wait in the living room while you are in the kitchen putting the finishing touches on the meal? Would you have dinner yourself and then give Him your leftovers at the end of the meal? Of course you wouldn't. Would you bring out the fine china and serve Him on your best dishes? Would you serve Him first? Would you be on time? Would you have everything prepared early, so He doesn't have to wait? Of course you would. It's the same with prayer.

By the end of the day, you may be weary and worn. It is so easy to get up, go to work or school, come home and do all the things we have to do around our homes (cooking, cleaning, bills, homework, returning phone calls/emails, etc.) before falling right back into bed again. And alas, another day passes without prayer and without ever having spent a moment of our day with the Lord. Don't give God your leftovers at the end of a hectic day.

We aren't saying you can't or shouldn't pray at the end of the day. What we are suggesting is that you set a regular time every day to spend with the Lord. Give Him your day before it starts. However, maybe the morning is just not the best time for you. Perhaps your most productive of prayers may be in the evening or bed time. That is just as great as the early birds praying in the morning.

I (Heather) love to pray at night before going to bed. As a matter of fact, just about as long as my husband and I have been married, we have been praying together at night before we go to bed. We also pray with our children before we put them to bed. When they are older, we plan to have a family time of prayer in the evening. It is good to close the day with the Lord. In Luke 6:12, NIV, it states that, "One of those days Jesus went out to a mountainside to pray, and spent the night praying."

Morning, noon or evening, you pick a time that is best for you. We are called to "pray without ceasing" (1 Thessalonians 5:17, NKJV). Therefore, we can and should be in a constant state of prayer regardless of the time. To put it simply, Jesus longs for us to pray!

Where

We suggest you find a spot, a location that is your personal, private place to spend with God. When I (Kim) pray, sometimes I pray out loud and sometimes I pray silently. I have found that I am a lot more focused when I pray out loud. Thus, if I am going to be praying out loud, I choose a place of solitude. "But you, when you pray, go into your room, and when you have shut your door, pray to your Father who is in the secret place; and your Father who sees in secret will reward you openly" (Matthew 6:6, NKJV). Your spot is your place for only you and God.

I (Heather) love nature! The times I am able to get alone in nature and pray to the Lord are my favorite times of prayer. I fill the closest to God then. A great friend of mine loves praying at the beach. I recall hearing numerous stories of her awesome prayer times while at the beach. You may have a favorite, comfy chair that you love climbing into as you have your prayer time. For years, I prayed on my way to school and now continue to do so on my way to work. So I must admit that my car is another place of prayer for me. Through high school, college and now in my career, I pray to the Lord before starting the day. I also love praying in my baby's nursery. There is such an awesome, angelic, pure feeling when I rock my baby at night and pray unto the Lord.

Find a place that makes you feel the closest to God. You may not always pick the same spot to pray, but whatever the location, get alone and feel the presence of God. Allow the Holy Spirit to flow through you as you speak to your heavenly Father in your place of prayer.

Why

You may be asking, "Why pray?" The reason is because prayer is our direct line of communication with our Heavenly Father. What is a relationship with Christ without communication? Not much of one at all. How great would your marriage be if you never spoke to each other? What about your relationships with your parents, friends and family? Without the interaction, the relationship would fail. The Lord loves us and longs to hear from us by our communicating with Him through prayer.

He has so many awesome things in store for our lives if only we would seek Him and discover what they are. How rewarding it must be for a parent to present their child with a gift on Christmas after having heard their child beg for it all year long. Surely, it brings them more delight to give their child that gift, than one the child never asked for in the first place. "If you then, being evil, know how to give good gifts to your children, how much more will your Father who is in heaven give good things to those who ask Him!" (Matthew 7:11, NKJV). God longs to give us the desires of our hearts but He wants to hear us talk to Him about them. "Delight yourself also in the Lord, and He shall give you the desires of your heart" (Psalms 37:4, NKJV).

Not only is prayer beneficial to our relationship with Christ because of our coming before Him with requests but it is also beneficial because prayer is our means of praising our Father and lifting up thanksgiving unto His name. Our earthly relationships are cultivated when we encourage and lift up one another. The same stands true with our relationship with Christ. If we can give Him nothing more than praise then let's start praising! Prayer is our main line of communication with our loving, Heavenly Father.

Exodus 15:2, NIV "The Lord is my strength and my song; he has become my salvation. He is my God, and I will praise him, my father's God, and I will exalt him."

Psalm 40:3, NIV "He put a new song in my mouth, a hymn of praise to our God. Many will see and fear and put their trust in the Lord."

PRAYER

Oh Heavenly Father, thank You for giving us the freedom to pray. Thank You for calling us by name and the yearning to hear from us through prayer. May we learn from You and Your examples of prayer through reading Your word. Thank You that we don't have to come before You with eloquent speech or proper grammar. We can come to You just as we are. May You teach us to pray without ceasing.

In Jesus name,
Amen

VERSES

Hebrews 12:1 (NKJV): "...run with endurance the race that is set before us."

Ecclesiastes 11:4 (TLB): "If you wait for the perfect conditions, you will never get anything done."

Who

John 3:16 (NIV): "God so loved the world that He gave His one and only son, that whoever believes in Him shall not perish but have eternal life."

John 14:26 (NIV): "But the Counselor, the Holy Spirit, whom the Father will send in my name, will teach you all things and will remind you of everything I have said to you."

John 1:12 (NIV): "As many as received Him, to them He gave the right to become children of God, even to those who believe in His name."

Romans 3:23 (NIV): "For all have sinned and fall short of the glory of God."

Romans 6:23 (NIV): "The wages of sin is death, but the gift of God is eternal life in Christ Jesus our Lord."

Ephesians 2:8-9 (NIV): "By grace you have been saved through faith; and that not of yourselves, it is the gift of God; not as a result of works that no one should boast."

Revelation 3:20 (NIV): "Behold, I stand at the door and knock; if any one hears My voice and opens the door, I will come in to him."

What

Matthew 6:9-13 (KJV): "Our Father which art in heaven, Hallowed be thy name. Thy kingdom come, thy will be done in earth, as it is in heaven. Give us this day our daily bread.

And forgive us our debts, as we forgive our debtors. And lead us not into temptation, but deliver us from evil: For thine is the kingdom, and the power, and the glory, for ever. Amen."

Matthew 6:7-8 (TLB): "Don't recite the same prayer over and over as the heathen do, who think prayers are answered only by repeating them again and again."

Philippians 4:6, (NKJV): "Be anxious for nothing, but in everything by prayer and supplication with thanksgiving, let your requests be made known to God."

John 14:13-14, (NKJV): "And whatever you ask in My name that I will do, that the Father may be glorified in the Son. If you ask anything in My name, I will do it."

John 16:23-24, (NKJV): "...Most assuredly, I say to you, whatever you ask the Father in My name He will give you. Until now you have asked nothing in My name. Ask, and you will receive, that your joy may be full."

When

Hebrews 12:11 (NIV): "No discipline seems pleasant at the time, but painful. Later on, however, it produces a harvest of righteousness and peace for those who have been trained by it."

Mark 1:35 (NIV): "Very early in the morning, while it was still dark, Jesus got up, left the house and went off to a solitary place, where He prayed."

Luke 6:12 (NIV): "One of those days Jesus went out to a mountainside to pray, and spent the night praying."

1 Thessalonians 5:17 (NKJV): "pray without ceasing"

Where

Matthew 6:6 (NKJV): "But you, when you pray, go into your room, and when you have shut your door, pray to your

Father who is in the secret place; and your Father who sees in secret will reward you openly."

Why

Matthew 7:11 (NKJV): "If you then, being evil, know how to give good gifts to your children, how much more will your Father who is in heaven give good things to those who ask Him."

Psalms 37:4 (NKJV): "Delight yourself also in the Lord, and He shall give you the desires of your heart."

Exodus 15:2 (NIV): "The Lord is my strength and my song; he has become my salvation. He is my God, and I will praise him, my father's God, and I will exalt him."

Psalm 40:3 (NIV): "He put a new song in my mouth, a hymn of praise to our God. Many will see and fear and put their trust in the Lord."

CHAPTER TWO

HOW?

In order to help with the "how" of praying, we have decided to give you a few tools that we think are helpful to assist you in praying. You can be as creative with them as you like or only use the suggestions that are most useful for you. Please don't feel that you have to try all suggestions, especially all at one time. We are just briefly touching on a few tools that we think can help jumpstart your prayer life. They have been very helpful to us in our personal prayer lives from time to time. Your prayer life is between you and God. You can use the tools to assist you or you can just simply pray. There are many people who never write one single journal entry, yet speak of their prayer life with such grace and boldness as if they have it memorized. Not everyone needs to journal. You may never desire to have quite as organized of a prayer life as we mention in this section. The idea is just to assist you in praying. As you read the next section, please don't get boggled down in the "how to." Just pray!

Begin with praises and thanksgiving

We suggest you begin your prayers with praise and thanksgiving. Philippians 4:6, NKJV, tells us to "Be anxious for nothing, but in everything by prayer and supplication with thanksgiving, let your requests be made known to God."

If you were to place all of the prayers that you have prayed over during the entire week into a big galvanized bucket, just how many cups full of praises to our Heavenly Father do you think you could pull out? We are talking about putting all of your weekly prayer time in there. These prayers could consist of praying on your way to work, praying while stuck in traffic, praying with your spouse and family at home, praying with friends, praying at church, your personal prayer time, etc. We mean *everything*. Every single time you come to the Lord put it in the bucket. We must be very transparent with you and unfortunately say that not even half of the bucket would be filled with praise if we were to do the same.

In order to look deep into praising the Father, come with us to the passage of Luke and learn about Jesus healing ten men with leprosy.

Luke 17:11-18, NIV:

"Now on his way to Jerusalem, Jesus traveled along the border between Samaria and Galilee. As he was going into a village, ten men who had leprosy met him. They stood at a distance and called out in a loud voice, "Jesus, Master, have pity on us!" When he saw them, he said, "Go, show yourselves to the priests." And as they went, they were cleansed. One of them, when he saw he was healed, came back, praising God in a loud voice. He threw himself at Jesus' feet and thanked him-and he was a Samaritan. Jesus asked, "Were not all ten cleansed? Where are the other nine? Was no one found to return and give praise to God except this foreigner?" Then he said to him, "Rise and go; your faith has made you well."

There were ten men with leprosy and only one decided to come back and give the Lord the praise He deserved. Let's look at this passage a little closer. It tells us that Jesus was on His way to Jerusalem. My (Heather) pastor, Mike Linch from NorthStar Church, once pointed out that if He was on His way to Jerusalem then He was on His way to the cross. Let's think about that for a moment. If He was on His way to Jerusalem then He was on His way to die on the cross for your sins, for my sins and also for the sins of the ten men with leprosy. As Mike pointed out, Jesus must have been very busy that day. He explained that Jesus' mind must have been full of what was about to come in His life just down the road, death on a cross. As busy as He was, He took the time to help these ten men with leprosy.

The passage also tells us that He took the route between Samaria and Galilee. Later on in the passage, Jesus points out that the one man who came back to praise Him was a foreigner, a Samaritan. History tells us that Jews and Samaritans were not the best of friends. In fact, Jews despised Samaritans. They thought Samaritans were not from pure descendants of Abraham like themselves, but were a mixed race due to intermarriages. What does all of that mean? It means that this guy was probably not voted "most popular" in the town. He was a minority, had leprosy and likely was down and discouraged at the time when his path crossed the path of Jesus. He alone returned to Jesus. Alone. He went against the flow and threw himself at the feet of Jesus.

Where did the other nine go? God's word doesn't tell us. Jesus himself even asked where the others were. They bolted. They were gone. They asked for their needs to be met. Jesus met their needs and they fled.

Where would we fall in those two categories? How many of us are just like the other nine? How often do we ask the Lord to hear our prayers, yet never thank Him and praise Him. Let's make a commitment right now to be like the one

Samaritan who stayed. He also got what he asked for but he came back to give Jesus the praise that was well deserved. He was the one who went against the grain.

Verse 16 tells us that he "threw himself at Jesus' feet and thanked him..." Jesus replied in verse 18 by telling us that no one was found to give praise to God but this one man. I assume by that statement that Jesus longs for our praise. He surely deserves it. Let's give Him the praise that is due His name. Let's change our prayer time to where we are not only asking for our needs and the needs of others to be met, but also spending time praising Jesus and thanking Him for all that He has done.

There are a number of ways in which we can praise Jesus. This can be very simple or very creative. Feel free to be as creative as the Holy Spirit leads you as you lift up praise and thanksgiving to our Heavenly Father. The following is a list of examples of ways to praise the name of the Lord:

~ Reading the names of God mentioned in His word (Maker, Creator, Healer, Comforter, Alpha, Omega, Prince of Peace, Abba Father, Yahweh, etc. or the Psalms are good starts)
~ Bible study, devotional books on the names of God
~ Singing or reciting praise songs
~ Writing a list of thanksgivings for the day
~ Taking a walk in nature and thanking Him for the nature surrounding you and all that He has given you

The previous list is only a few of the numerous ways you can praise the name of Jesus. He is amazing and deserves our praise. We think dying on the cross for the sins of the world certainly qualifies Him for a great deal of praise and thanksgiving.

Your prayers

You can come before the Lord to pray about anything and everything. We include many stories of things we've prayed for over the years in part two of this book. You can pray for anything, be it big or small. Over the years, we've prayed for our families, friends, relationships, jobs, moving, traveling, safety, finances, healing, our nation, strangers and the list goes on.

Ending your prayers

When ending your prayers, end with the phrase, "In Jesus name." In John 14:13-14, NKJV, Jesus says, "And whatever you ask in My name that I will do, that the Father may be glorified in the Son. If you ask anything in My name, I will do it." John 16:23-24, NKJV, He states, "...Most assuredly, I say to you, whatever you ask the Father in My name He will give you. Until now you have asked nothing in My name. Ask, and you will receive, that your joy may be full."

I remember one time I called Heather to pray for me. Unbeknownst to me, she was driving around at the Atlanta airport to pick up a friend. After I told her my prayer request, she prayed the following,

Father God
IN JESUS NAME I PRAY,
AMEN!

I was a little dumbfounded. Did I just have a lapse of memory? Did time pass so fast that I didn't get a chance to hear her prayers for me? Did I miss the bulk of the prayer? So I said, rather dumbfounded, "Uhmm, Heather, did you forget to *actually pray* for me?" At which point she responded that as she began her prayer for me a car suddenly pulled out in front of her, startling her and she had to abruptly end the prayer. It was quite amusing to say the least. All to say, that we try to be consistent in ending our prayers with "In Jesus name," regardless of the circumstances.

Getting ready to pray

1. Journal

Men and women of the World War I and II eras can definitely relate to soldier stories. We can only imagine that many soldiers were able to capture their love and endearment by putting their true feelings down on paper. At times, this was their only means of communication. It must have been touching to get a love letter from your beloved who was off fighting for our country. It was as if he was right there beside you as you were reading those words of endearment. It was a sense of closeness and togetherness that could be felt. Those letters allowed soldiers to communicate their true feelings when they were not able to see their loved one face to face or speak to them over the phone.

We too, have the ability to experience the same thing with our Heavenly Father. Just like the above mentioned soldier, we can capture our thoughts and prayers to our Father by putting our words on paper through journaling. When we journal, we write out the thoughts we feel God is communicating to us. It may be in regards to the sermon we heard that day, a deep conversation we've had with someone about God or a trial or situation we are going through. It may also be a prayer for someone else.

It's a good idea to put the date and possibly the time when you are journaling. We can't tell you how many times (no pun intended!) we've found out later, that prayers we've prayed were answered at the exact moment we were praying for them. It's good for you to go back, re-read your requests and write the dates they were answered as further testament to God's faithfulness. Prayers are answered sometimes instantaneously, sometimes the next day or in some cases, not until many years later. Regardless, you'll always have your journal to refer back to and see how your relationship with God has grown. Your journal is your personal communication with God.

In Habakkuk 2:2, TLB the Lord said, "...write my answer on a billboard, large and clear, so that anyone can read it at a glance and rush to tell others." There are places throughout this book that we will share with you copies of stories from our journals. Journaling is like a deep part of your soul. It's where you and your feelings alone reside. It's your personal talks and intimate conversations with the Lord who hears and answers your prayers. Journaling is your words spoken to God alone.

2. Prayer box

Another tool you may find helpful is to use a prayer box. Before making my (Heather's) prayer box, I felt as if I had an entire list of prayer requests and people to pray for. I felt as if I was never really able to focus on each request and give each request the time it deserved because I had so many to get through each night. My list was so long that at times, I would start praying, fall asleep, wake up again, fall asleep, wake up and start praying over a new request. This would go on and on until I realized it was morning. (You are laughing because you are just as guilty, right?) So are you eager to know more about a prayer box and how to use it? Read on!

Ingredients:
Recipe card box
Index cards
Pen/Pencils

Directions:

Feel free to decorate your prayer box as much or as little as you want. It is yours and will be your companion. You can put stickers on it, draw on it, write names on it or just leave it in the condition it was when you bought it.

The next step is to take your prayer list/request and put them one by one on their own index card. What was helpful for me was to start with family members. I would have an individual card for my immediate family and write their requests on the cards as well as the date I started praying over each request. As for extended family, I would have a index card for each family name. For example, my Aunt Patsy's entire family had their card titled "Dixons" (their last name.) I would put everyone in that family on one card and any requests I had for them. I did this for all of my extended family.

I made an index card for each friend that I prayed for and would fill it with prayer requests and dates. I would have a card for my Bible study group, Sunday school class, etc. I made a card for my country and leaders. I made a card for myself and all of my personal requests. Anything and every-thing I prayed over was placed on a card.

After making all of my cards, I divided them into six different days. I placed the cards under a certain day, Monday through Saturday. I left Sunday open for a day of praise and thanksgiving. Instead of going over a list of prayer requests on Sundays, I simply used that day for worship through reading over praises in Psalms or Proverbs, listening to or singing praise music, etc. in order to lift up praises to Jesus.

Once you have your prayer box organized and each request filed under a certain day, you will be able to focus on each request for that particular day and give it the time you feel it deserves without rushing through a list of a hundred different requests. For example on Monday you will only pull out Monday's requests and pray over those cards. However, if there is a necessity that you need to pray over on that day other than what is on your cards, do not feel like you can only pray over what is under Monday.

We do not desire for this tool or any other tool to become legalistic at all. They are simply ways to aide you in having a deeper prayer life. The prayer cards are so neat to have to look back on and see what prayers have been answered and when. As previously mentioned I always put dates beside my requests and then put the date on which they were answered. It is always so unbelievably encouraging to see how God has worked and answered the very prayers that you prayed. We hope that the prayer box will be a wonderful tool to assist you to a more organized, more meaningful prayer life.

3. Memorizing Scripture/Verses

Joshua 1:8 (NKJV): "This Book of the Law shall not depart from your mouth, but you shall meditate in it day and night, that you may observe to do according to all this is written in it. For then you will make your way prosperous, and then you will have good success."

Hebrews 4:12 (NKJV): "For the word of God is living and powerful, sharper than any two-edged sword, piercing even to the division of soul and spirit, and of joint and marrow, and is a discerner of the thoughts and intent of the heart."

John 15:7 (NKJV): "If you abide in Me and My words abide in you, you will ask what you desire and it shall be done for you."

How many songs have you memorized since, oh say, the year 2000? Too numerous to count?? If you are like us, just about every other song that comes on your favorite radio station, you are able to bop your head along with and sing the tune just as if you were up on stage performing it yourself. Or what about the winning teams of the Super Bowl and World Series over the last decade? Can you name the classic sports moments of such events? The point we are trying to make here is that we can so easily remember songs, sporting events or any other pop culture event. So why is it much harder for us to commit to memorizing the scriptures and love stories that our Heavenly Father wrote with us in mind? For most of us, John 3:16 is the only verse we can just blurt out at the drop of a hat. For the sake of blurting, let's all say it aloud together. John 3:16, NIV, "For God so loved the world that He gave His one and only Son, that whoever believes in Him shall not perish but have eternal life."

I (Heather) will never forget the first verse I ever memorized. I was in eleventh grade. My family and I did not attend church regularly when I was a child. I did not have the privilege of going to Vacation Bible School or Awanas (a children's program with emphasis on scripture memorization) in order to begin memorizing scripture at an early age. It wasn't until high school that I attended church on a regular basis, and that is thanks to my high school best friend Missy. She invited me to her church and Sunday school class. Her class had been working on memorizing John 10:10, NIV, "The thief comes only to steal and kill and destroy; I have come that they may have life, and have it to the full." That day when you got to the classroom door, you had to quote the verse to the Sunday school teacher, Woody, or else you had to sit on the other side of the room. I was so embarrassed because I had never tried to memorize that verse or any verse. Thank the Lord, he was a compassionate teacher and allowed me to quote John 3:16 instead. I barely even knew John 3:16. But I tell you what, to this very day, I can tell you John 10:10 practically backwards and forwards. For humoring purposes, I will tell it to you backwards. Full the to it have and, life have may they that come have I; destroy and kill and steal to only comes thief the.

That was my first encounter with scripture memorization and it helped ignite a spark within my soul that has led me to memorize a plethora of scripture since that day. I must confess that I currently need a little kick to get me once again motivated to memorize scripture. I need to make it a lifetime commitment. Maybe I should go back to Mr. Woody's Sunday school class in order to get that jumpstart that I once again need.

We recommend that you memorize scripture on a regular basis. Pick a verse that you feel God has laid on your heart. Set a goal. For instance, pick a verse and spend one week to memorize it. Maybe you don't know where to get started. If that's the case, we have a list of verses at the end of every chapter that may help you with scripture memorization. We recommend memorizing scripture from Psalms and Proverbs. Memorize Psalms to provide you with encouragement and Proverbs to provide you with wisdom.

One reason scripture memorization is so vital to establishing a richer prayer life is because you can recite scripture in your prayers. Isaiah 55:11, NIV, tells us that our words that go out from our mouths will not return to us empty. The New King James Version uses the word, "void" instead of empty. When speaking the word of the Lord, our words are real and true. They will not return unto us void. Let's claim the words of Jesus!

For example, when you are praying for healing for someone, it is awesome to be able to pray unto the Lord using words that He gave us in His word regarding healing. According to 1 Peter 2:24b (NIV), "... by His wounds you have been healed." If you or someone that you are praying for is faced with a great deal of anxiety, then you could easily pray over the request by claiming Psalm 139:23, NIV,

"Search me, Oh God, and know my heart; test me and know my anxious thoughts." What better way to pray unto the Lord than by reciting and claiming the promises that He already gave us in advance.

Additionally, scripture memorization is vital when you are praying and seeking out the Lord's guidance for your life. When you have something memorized, it is amazing how swiftly that verse comes to mind in your time of need to give you the answer. The scriptures that were written so many years ago continue to be completely applicable in today's world. Do not be deceived into thinking that the answers aren't in the Book, because they most assuredly are.

TIP: We spoke earlier of prayer boxes. One suggestion is to keep your memory cards in your prayer box and each day/night that you take out your set of prayers for that day, you can also take out a set of memory cards and practice memorizing them.

4. Books

God speaks to us through His word. Job 32:8, NKJV, states "But there is a spirit in man, and the breath of the Almighty gives him understanding." The Bible offers knowledge. It is our guidebook for life and a wealth of information. In Matthew 4:4, TLB, Jesus says, "...For the Scriptures tell us that bread won't feed men's souls: obedience to every word of God is what we need." 2 Timothy 3:16-17, NIV, "All scripture is God-breathed and is useful for teaching, rebuking, correcting and training in righteousness, so that the man of God may be thoroughly equipped for every good work." The word of God is real. Every question that we would ever want answered is found in God's word, the Bible. We encourage you to be in God's word on a daily basis.

In addition to the Bible, we recommend filling your heart and mind with those things that edify your walk with Christ. Proverbs 4:23 (NIV), "Above all else, guard your heart, for it is the wellspring of life." If you are addicted to or interested in distasteful literature and that's all you read, then that will control your thoughts and thus your prayer life. If you spend the majority of your time filling your mind with that which is not beneficial and edifying then it will be really hard for you to have a completely focused and purposeful prayer life. 2 Corinthians 10:5, NIV, tells us that we are to "...demolish arguments and every pretension that sets itself up against the knowledge of God and take captive every thought to make it obedient to Christ." Another verse that teaches us how to fill our minds and thoughts is Philippians 4:8, NIV, "Finally, brethren, whatever is true, whatever is honorable, whatever is right, whatever is pure, whatever is lovely, whatever is of good repute, if there is any excellence and if anything worthy of praise, dwell on these things." Whatever you put into your mind will eventually surface its way out.

We have learned so much through the Christian books that the Lord has led us to read. Many aspects of books we've read have been vital in inspiring our lives and strengthening our walks with Christ. It is our prayer that even this very book will be added to your list of books that have been an instrument in edifying your life and will help you on your journey of prayer. We believe in prayer and will claim the promise that PRAYER WORKS!

PRAYER

Heavenly Father,

You are our Maker and Creator. You are the beginning and the end. Without You we are nothing. O how praise is due Your Holy name. Thank You for dying on the cross for our sins. Thank You for loving us unconditionally. Thank You for choosing us to be your children. You made the earth and saw that it was good. Thank You for creating nature to be so beautiful for us to enjoy. We praise You for Your word and all that we are able to learn from it. Thank You for our family and friends. Thank You for all that You have given to us and will continue to do in our lives. We praise You and lift Your name on high. You are our comforter, our strength, our healer, our helper in times of need. You alone are our everything. Above all nations and kings, we praise your name, O Lord.

I come before You and ask You to show me how to use the various means described to edify my own prayer life. I pray that You will help me to become diligent and disciplined in my prayer life. I know that You can do wonderful things through prayer. I pray that You will teach me how to grow in my walk with You.

I pray that You will give me the discipline to set aside a time every single day to be alone with You in prayer. I pray that You will grow in me a sense of faith that You can do amazing things in and through prayer. I pray that You will remind me of your ability to do the humanly impossible. I come before You now and ask You to work in the impossible situations in my life. I pray that You will align my will with Your will for my life. I pray that You be in charge of every area of my life and guide me. I pray that You develop in me the fruit of the Spirit and help deepen my relationship with You.

In Jesus name,
Amen

VERSES

Philippians 4:6 (NKJV): "Be anxious for nothing, but in everything by prayer and supplication with thanksgiving, let your requests be made known to God."

John 14:13-14 (NKJV): "And whatever you ask in My name that I will do, that the Father may be glorified in the Son. If you ask anything in My name, I will do it."

John 16:23-24 (NKJV): "...Most assuredly, I say to you, whatever you ask the Father in My name He will give you. Until now you have asked nothing in My name. Ask, and you will receive, that your joy may be full."

Habakkuk 2:2 (TLB): "...write my answer on a billboard, large and clear, so that anyone can read it at a glance and rush to tell others."

Joshua 1:8 (NKJV): "This Book of the Law shall not depart from your mouth, but you shall meditate in it day and night, that you may observe to do according to all this is written in it. For then you will make your way prosperous, and then you will have good success."

Hebrews 4:12 (NKJV): "For the word of God is living and powerful, sharper than any two-edged sword, piercing even to the division of soul and spirit, and of joint and marrow, and is a discerner of the thoughts and intent of the heart."

John 15:7 (NKJV): "If you abide in Me and My words abide in you, you will ask what you desire and it shall be done for you

John 3:16 (NIV): "For God so loved the world that He gave His one and only Son, that whoever believes in Him shall not perish but have eternal life."

John 10:10 (NIV): "The thief comes only to steal and kill and destroy; I have come that they may have life, and have it to the full."

Isaiah 55:11 (NIV): "so is my word that goes out from my mouth; It will not return to me empty, but will accomplish what I desire and achieve the purpose for which I sent it."

Isaiah 55:11 (NKJV): "So shall my word be that goes forth from My mouth; It shall not return to Me void, but it will accomplish what I please, and it shall prosper in the thing for which I sent it."

1 Peter 2:24b (NIV), "… by His wounds you have been healed."

Psalm 139:23 (NIV): "Search me, Oh God, and know my heart; test me and know my anxious thoughts."

Job 32:8 (NKJV): "But there is a spirit in man, and the breath of the Almighty gives him understanding."

Matthew 4:4 (TLB): "...For the Scriptures tell us that bread won't feed men's souls: obedience to every word of God is what we need."

2 Timothy 3:16-17 (NIV): "All scripture is God-breathed and is useful for teaching, rebuking, correcting and training in righteousness, so that the man of God may be thoroughly equipped for every good work."

Proverbs 4:23 (NIV): "Above all else, guard your heart, for it is the wellspring of life."

2 Corinthians 10:5 (NIV): "...demolish arguments and every pretension that sets itself up against the knowledge of God and take captive every thought to make it obedient to Christ."

Philippians 4:8 (NIV): "Finally, brethren, whatever is true, whatever is honorable, whatever is right, whatever is pure, whatever is lovely, whatever is of good repute, if there is any excellence and if anything worthy of praise, dwell on these things."

CHAPTER THREE

BEGINNER, INTERMEDIATE, ADVANCED

Here's our jumpstart to prayer. You may be pondering several questions. Prayer?!? Where do I even begin? Where am I headed in my prayer life? Where will I end up? Will I ever be a "prayer warrior"? Do not worry or be anxious, my friend. Our loving, Heavenly Father desires exactly that for you. It may take time to cultivate the characteristics of an in depth prayer life. With patience, diligence and the faith to trust God as He moves you, you will be well on your way to developing a deeper prayer life.

As you read along, the next section is designed to give a brief overview of how we've chosen to explain three levels of a prayer life. You may want to know how to move ahead and deepen your prayer life. Some of you may be at the beginning and desire to get on the track of becoming a prayer warrior. We divided this into three different stages, beginning, intermediate and advanced. We invite you to continue reading and explore all these have to offer. May they encourage you to grow in Christ in the area of prayer.

Beginner Level

The beginner level of a prayer life is more of an individualized level. A person who is at this level has not ever really had a daily prayer life. The best way to get started is to make a commitment to pray daily for an entire month. Pick a time that is most convenient for you and stick with it. (If you are truly just starting out, you may not want to pray at night in your bed as you are falling asleep. Believe us, you will often fall asleep and never finish your conversation with the Lord.)

As mentioned in Chapter Two, journaling is a great tool to help cultivate a daily prayer life. It is a great motivator to help you continue praying when you are able to look back and see how the Lord answered your prayers.

If you feel comfortable enough, you may want to begin praying aloud. This will help prepare you for praying aloud in groups. We know that may seem a long way away for some of you, but we promise the Lord will lead you to that level when the time is right. We also encourage you to begin memorizing scripture if you have never done so. You may refer to our "Memorizing Scripture" section for extra guidance in this area. As we mentioned in that section, scripture memorization is a great tool to use as you pray to the Lord. It is awesome to quote scripture to the Lord. Claim His promises as you pray.

If you are just beginning on your journey of prayer, be encouraged. You are on the road to seeing wonderful miracles right before your very eyes. Start small and advance as you feel the Holy Spirit leading you. As mentioned earlier, the best way to get started is to just start praying. Set aside time every single day for prayer. As you move forward, with the Lord leading you, you will begin to realize that prayer becomes a natural part of your every day life.

The Lord has blessed all of us with the freedom to pray anywhere and at anytime. WOW! Regardless of our busy schedules or what we have going on in the day, we can pray. Your prayer time can be as you drive to work in the morning. What a great way to start your day and turn it over to the Lord. You can even make a trip to the grocery store or shopping mall a time of prayer. As you go down the aisle picking out your milk and bread, why not use that alone time to pray through your prayer requests for yourself and others?

My road trip friend and I (Heather) often used our time traveling in the car for prayer. At the beginning of each hour, we would spend several minutes in prayer. We prayed together out loud, but if you do not yet feel comfortable praying aloud with someone else, you can still use this idea and pray quietly to yourself. However, please remember that if you are going to have a prayer time while driving in your car...you need to keep your eyes open. The Lord will understand.

These are just a few ideas of places and times you can pray. The list could go on and on. The point is simply that there is a time when we need to get quiet before the Lord and set aside a time to pray. However, we can also "pray without ceasing" (1 Thessalonians 5:17, KJV) in just about any location and at any time.

We encourage you and are praying for you as you begin your very own, special journey of prayer! Prayer works. The Lord is calling you "..for such a time as this" to pray (Esther 4:14b, NIV).

PRAYER

Oh Lord,

We come before You now to pray for our readers, who feel as if they are at the beginner level of their prayer life. We are so excited that You have called them to pray. We pray over their time with You and steadfastness as they seek a deeper prayer life. May You change their life through prayer! An awesome road of prayer lies before them. Oh Lord, we lift them up to You and ask that You lead them in their new journey of prayer.

In Jesus name,
Amen

Intermediate Level

Once you are comfortable in your daily prayer time with the Lord, you may feel that it is time for you to kick your prayer life up a notch. This is the perfect time for you to begin praying with another person, a prayer partner. Begin by praying for the needs of others. "Let us then approach the throne of grace with confidence, so that we may receive mercy and find grace to help us in our time of need" (Hebrews 4:16, NIV). Go before the Lord on their behalf. You may also begin praying for the impossible. This means pray over matters that are completely out of your control. It means praying for things that you know *only* God can answer. "But Jesus looked at them and said to them, 'With men this is impossible, but with God all things are possible" (Matthew 19:26, NKJV).

God calls His people to pray and desires for us to grow in the area of prayer. It is not about the words that you use when you pray, rather it is about your heart. Romans 8:26

(NIV) tells us, "…We do not know what we ought to pray for, but the Spirit himself intercedes for us…." God's word tell us, "…He who searches our hearts knows the mind of the Spirit, because the Spirit intercedes for the saints in accordance with God's will" (Romans 8:27, NIV). As you grow in your prayer life, you will become more and more comfortable praying (interceding) for others and deepening your prayer life.

Prayer Partners

Praying together with another and in groups is mentioned numerous times throughout the Bible. God calls us to pray with other believers. Many prayers have been answered as a result of a group of believers praying together. This group could consist of two or more people. Matthew 18:19-20, NIV, tells us that "if two of you on earth agree about anything you ask for, it will be done for you by my Father in Heaven. For where two or three come together in my name, there I am in the midst of them."

Having a prayer partner necessitates you sharing the events in your life. You need to have a person or people you feel comfortable talking to, about things that are personal to you. A prayer partner is someone who maintains your confidentiality regarding personal prayer matters. He or she should look to the scripture to encourage you and help hold you accountable for your actions. He or she must be willing to help you grow in your faith and walk with the Lord and vice versa. Once you each discuss your life issues and what you are struggling with, worried about or want to overcome, then you can pray for one another over them. We encourage you to pray over both the big and small issues. God hears all of your prayers. We encourage you to come before the Lord with others to pray and experience all that God has for you through this.

How touching and tender it is to have people in your life that can and will pray for you. It is moving to be in the presence of someone who talks to God about you, in your presence. More often than not, when Heather prays for me (or vice versa) once the prayer is over, I will ask, "How did you *know* that?" Upon which her response is usually, "I didn't." She prays over what comes to mind at that moment. A lot of times she will pray for something I never mentioned to her and that she knows nothing about, be it a word, phrase or sentence that comes to mind. This is the Holy Spirit bringing things to mind during our prayers. It is even more reassurance that there is a God, a God who hears our prayers and knows before we do what our needs are. This is not mere coincidence that this happens, it is God.

It is very encouraging to have another person to pray with so that you "...may spur one another on toward love and good deeds" (Hebrews 10:24, NIV).

Heather's Thoughts

Although I didn't have a deep understanding of the Lord as a child, I always had the desire to pray. It was as if the Lord "wooed" me and drew me to Himself. My prayers were very simple and childlike. Matthew 21:16b (NIV), "From the lips of children's and infants, You have ordained praise."

As I continued to pray as a child and my prayer life was strengthened, I began to pray for my family, asking the Lord to keep us safe and protected. I would ask Him to watch over my mommy, daddy and family members. Though as children, we may not understand the entire depth of prayer, I believe God hears the cries and outpours of children. To me, there is nothing sweeter than hearing a child pray. They are simple and straight to the point. I love hearing my children pray before bedtime. It is so sweet to hear them pray aloud for each other and our family. Through their prayers,

I am reminded of the precious simplicity of my childhood prayers.

As I grew older, my walk with the Lord and my understanding of prayer began to increase substantially. I began to understand the importance of prayer and that it was my direct line to communicate with my Heavenly Father. My prayer life was strengthened the most when I moved away to college. College is a big transition for most of us. During those years, many young adults try and figure out who they are and what they believe. During this time in my life, I clung to Jesus and held fast to Him. My walk with the Lord grew deeper and deeper during my years in college. It helped that I found a good church with an excellent college ministry and surrounded myself with other believers who encouraged me and uplifted my walk with Christ.

I had several friends whom I considered partners in prayer during college. My friend Tammy and I cultivated our friendship as a result of prayer. One summer, we decided to get together every single day to pray for our families. We made a list of every person in our families (both immediate and extended) and committed to pray together for them daily. Sometimes it would be two AM when we got together to pray or 6:30 in the morning before we began our day. Time was not an obstacle. We were committed that summer to pray for our families on a daily basis. We both believe God did awesome things in our families lives that summer and is still at work as a result of our uplifted cries unto Him. She is now a lifelong friend of mine and that friendship was truly enriched over a summer of praying together.

Kim's Thoughts

> *Proverbs 27:17, NKJV states, "As iron sharpens iron, so a man sharpens the countenance of his friend."*

One night, I was speaking to Heather about a problem I was having. She asked if we could stop right then and if she could pray for me over the issue. Then she prayed aloud for me. I remember thinking that I'd like to be comfortable enough to pray out loud for someone at a moment's notice. It wasn't long after that we decided to start praying together.

We were initially in the same town and could meet together in person. There came a point when we both moved, yet we wanted to remain faithful in praying. I remember we would telephone each other at 5:30 am every morning before our days began in order to come to the Lord in prayer. We developed a sense of discipline in our prayer lives that has continued. It certainly was not easy to be awake, alert and prayerful so early in the morning. Yet Hebrews 12:11, NKJV, tells us that "now no chastening seems to be joyful for the present, but painful; nevertheless, afterwards it yields the peaceable fruit of righteousness to those who have been trained by it." The Bible speaks of this fruit. Galatians 5:22-23a (NKJV) says, "...the fruit of the Spirit is love, joy, peace, longsuffering, kindness, goodness, faithfulness, gentleness, self control..."

That was over a decade ago and we are still praying together today. I don't think either one of us ever imagined we'd still be praying together after so many years. However, praise the Lord for cell phones with free long distance, as we've been on different sides of the country or the world during this time. We've logged many an hour on the phone in prayer and accountability. It has been an incredible journey for each of us. We've grown tremendously in our faith and trust in the Lord over this period of time. As Hebrews 12:1, NKJV tells us we are to "....Run with endurance the race that is set before us."

There are many different ways for a prayer partnership to work. The way that we decided and continue to make our partnership work, is to make a list of prayer requests for ourselves and then have the other one pray over it. It is not always a lengthy list, usually five to ten requests at most. We both make a copy of each others requests and commit ourselves to pray over them. These requests consist of a variety of things. We pray for our families, friends, our future, finances, specific needs in our lives at that particular time and the list goes on and on. We pray over these requests and then get back together in order to update and change them quarterly. We either pray in person or over the phone if distance doesn't allow us to meet in person.

We encourage you as you grow in your prayer life and walk with the Lord. We ask that you wait and see. He is ready to do amazing things in and through your life! Remember, my friend, prayer is not only about asking, but it is also about trusting and believing.

PRAYER

Heavenly Father,

We come before You and pray for our friends and their hunger to grow deeper in the area of prayer. If it is time and the Spirit is stirring in their hearts for them to seek out a prayer partner/accountability partner for themselves, then we trust that You will lead them to the right person at the right time. May they become more and more in tune with the needs of others. May the Spirit stir their hearts to pray for the needs of others. Help them to begin using scripture in their prayers. May You bring verses to their minds as they pray so they can return Your word unto You in prayer. May they grow in the area of prayer and daily trust You more and more. You call us to pray and long to do amazing things in our lives as a result of having heard our hearts cry out to You. Hear us, O Lord. Move us and call us to pray.

It is in Your precious name, Jesus, that we pray,
Amen

Advanced Level

Are you the first person that comes to mind when someone has a need or prayer request? Do others often come to you and ask for you to take a moment to pray with them over a concerning matter? Are you diligent in prayer and people trust you to pray over their needs. What a compliment. What an encouragement. We praise the Lord for your desire to pray. We pray that you will be encouraged to stand up with us and desire to lead others in the area of prayer. We like to call those of you who fall into this category, "prayer warriors."

There is a country western song about praying for others. My friend Shannon greatly encouraged me (Heather) when she told me that song made her think of me. She explained that if there is ever a need in her life she could always put faith in me to pray for her. WOW. The thought that she would trust me to approach the throne of our Savior on her behalf was not only encouraging but humbling for me. That statement only encouraged me to be more serious about prayer and more diligent in my prayers for others when they came to me with a need or request.

As you advance in the area of prayer, you will likely feel more and more comfortable praying aloud in front of a group, speaking at a Bible study about prayer or even writing a book on prayer. We pray that you will have the confidence to pray in front of others. The Lord made us each with very unique personalities and some of you may not ever feel comfortable praying aloud in front of a group. However, if the Spirit calls, we encourage you to be bold. Step outside of your comfort zone. Stand up for our Savior and pray.

As a prayer warrior, you may also desire to speak to others about prayer and let them know how awesome it is to have a strong prayer life. As previously mentioned, there are so many different ways to strengthen your own prayer life, while encouraging others along their journey. If a family member, friend or co-worker has a need, stop that very second and pray with them. Not only are you going to the Father over their needs at that very moment, but you are being a leader in the area of prayer. You are opening up the door for that person to see God work through prayer.

We desire to encourage you as you grow in your prayer walk. Be steadfast, my friend, an awesome journey lies ahead. Remember that He promises us that we are able to "….approach the throne of grace with confidence…." (Hebrews 4:16, NIV).

PRAYER

Oh Father,

We approach the throne of grace with confidence as we pray over our fellow prayer warriors. May they continue to seek You, continue to hunger and thirst for more of You and may they continue praying. You have heard their cries and have been faithful to answer their requests. May they be encouraged daily as they too approach the throne of grace with much confidence. Use them and their prayer journey to encourage others to pray.

In Jesus name we pray,
Amen

VERSES

1 Thessalonians 5:17 (KJV): "pray without ceasing"

Romans 8:26-27 (NIV): "In the same way, the Spirit helps us in our weakness. We do not know what we ought to pray for, but€ the Spirit himself intercedes for us with groans that words cannot express. And he who searches our hearts knows the mind of the Spirit, because the Spirit intercedes for the saints in accordance with God's will."

Esther 4:14b (NIV): "...for such a time as this."

Hebrews 4:16 (NIV): "Let us then approach the throne of grace with confidence, so that we may receive mercy and find grace to help us in our time of need."

Matthew 19:26 (NKJV): "But Jesus looked at them and said to them, 'With men this is impossible, but with God all things are possible"

Romans 8:26 (NIV) tells us, "...We do not know what we ought to pray for, but the Spirit himself intercedes for us...."

Romans 8:27 (NIV): "..he who searches our hearts knows the mind of the Spirit, because the Spirit intercedes for the saints in accordance with God's will."

Matthew 18:19-20 (NKJV): "...if two of you on earth agree about anything you ask for, it will be done for you by my Father in Heaven. For where two or three come together in my name, there I am in the midst of them."

Hebrews 10:24 (NIV): "And let us consider how we may spur one another on toward love and good deeds."

Matthew 21:16b (NIV): "From the lips of children's and infants, You have ordained praise."

Proverbs 27:17 (NKJV): "As iron sharpens iron, so a man sharpens the countenance of his friend."

Hebrews 12:11 (NKJV): "now no chastening seems to be joyful for the present, but painful; nevertheless, afterwards it yields the peaceable fruit of righteousness to those who have been trained by it."

Galatians 5:22-23a (NKVJ): "But the fruit of the Spirit is love, joy, peace, longsuffering, kindness, goodness, faithfulness, gentleness, self control..."

Hebrews 12:1 (NKJV): "....Run with endurance the race that is set before us."

CHAPTER FOUR

THE LORD ALWAYS HAS AN ANSWER: YES, NO OR WAIT

Can we all agree that more times than not, the Lord answers our prayers? Actually, He always answers them. Yes, always. He answers them but the answers may not be the answer we were praying for. They may not be answered when or how we think they should be answered. Yet, He always gives us an answer to our prayers. Yes, no or wait.

We have instant gratification and rejoice when the Lord answers our heart's cries immediately with the answer yes. The timing must have been right. He works in amazing ways and His ways are perfect. When He answers yes, it is usually because the request was in alignment with what the Lord desired for us at that moment. It was in His plan to hear and answer that request at that specified time. God is good. Praise Him for the times that He hears us and answers our desires immediately.

Yet, praise Him for the times that He says no or wait. Why? Why would we rejoice when the Lord says no or wait? It is because those are the times that we are stretched, strengthened and grow the most. Have you ever longed for something and the more you waited for it the more you grew to love it? Think about your dream car. Had you went out and bought it the second you desired it, the gratification would not have been as intense had you waited and saved up your money and purchased the car after a great deal of time had passed. Sometimes the Lord says no and other times He says wait. Nonetheless, He always answers.

Is the answer, No?

We want you to know that the Lord loves you and only has your best interest in mind. He only wants the best for you. He loves you that much. If He answers a request with no, it is for a reason. It may be difficult to have Him answer with no, but it is for your best.

Years ago when I was much younger my path crossed with a certain guy and soon after we met, I felt like the Lord impressed upon my heart that I was going to marry him. "Marry him?" I asked. "I don't even know him." It was a very strange feeling, one that I will never forget. I thought I was pretty good at discerning God's will and this idea was absolutely crazy, but I really felt that the Lord was telling me that I was to marry this guy. We became very good friends over the next several years but never dated. All along I felt that I was to marry him. By the end of our friendship he was dating a wonderful girl and was at the point of proposing to her. At the same time, I was about to move from that town to another location. Neither of those things mattered to me; I continued to feel that I was to marry him.

Kim and I decided to do some serious praying. We prayed hard, you know, the get on your knees and pray kind of praying? O, Lord how do I know if this is You? I needed a sign and that is exactly what I prayed for. We prayed for a certain sign and opened the word of God. I felt the Lord call me to pray for the word "wings." I had no idea why.

We randomly flipped open the Bible and the scripture that it landed on was in Isaiah, describing in great depths the wings of angels. Wow! We were taken aback. Was this from the Lord? Was I truly hearing His voice? Was this my sign? Weeks passed and he was still planning on marrying his girlfriend. Weeks passed and I still believed that I was to marry him.

The day that I was to move, I once again prayed for the same sign. As the truck pulled away with all of my belongings I stuck around to deal with a few odds and ends. There on the pavement lay a little piece of paper. I had seen the paper all day but never really thought to pick it up. I don't know what made me pick it up this time but I was shocked at what I read. It was one of those little "pass it on" notes with an eagle on it. It had scripture on it from Isaiah 40:31, NIV, "But those who hope in the Lord will renew their strength. They will soar on wings like eagles; they will run and not grow weary, they will walk and not be faint." Again, I was in awe of what I had just read. I was to the point of shaking. Actually, I threw the note down on the ground because I was in such shock. Once again the same thought crossed my mind. Was this truly from the Lord? Was I really supposed to marry this guy? I was so confused. I was days from moving away and he was days from getting engaged. Why in the world did I feel this way? Yet all along, as I prayed, I felt as though the Lord continued to tell me that I was to marry him.

To make a long, drawn out drama of a story short, I didn't marry him. I know, I know. As you read you were thinking that we lived "happily ever after." Well he ended up marrying his wonderful, godly girlfriend. In the years to follow, I married my own prince charming. I may never know what that was all about this side of heaven, but what I do know is I learned a lot through it. I was stretched and strengthened more than I could have imagined. That story was very real to me and very personal. I really can't explain on paper all that I went through during that time in my life. I thought I heard the voice of God, yet in the end He said, "No." Why did I go through all of that to have that end result? Looking back, maybe all along, the Lord was telling me to wait on His timing, but the answer to this particular request was No! It was such a hard time for me. I was devastated at the time. It took me a long time after that to trust that I had a lick of discernment at all. I never stopped trusting the Lord but I stopped trusting how I heard Him. It took me a long time to be able to trust who I was in Christ.

All did end up well. As I have already mentioned, I am happily married and adore my husband. He brings me more joy than imaginable. I can say that now, but at the time God answered "No" to my request, I was devastated. "No" is not always easy. Yet it is always for the best. God only has the best in store for our lives. We must trust God amidst His No's.

When the Lord says wait

At times, the Lord tells us to wait. This is usually because you are not ready or the other end of your request is not ready. Are you praying for your mate and wanting more than anything for him or her to come into your life? Would you want God to do that before both of you were ready? You wouldn't have the marriage that God desired for you if the time came before both of you were ready. It is easy to get ahead of God, but we must learn that His timing is perfect. Times of waiting are usually difficult to bear. However, we are often stretched and strengthened beyond our imagination when God takes us through a waiting period.

How do you think Jacob felt when he had to wait on the Lord's perfect timing in order to marry his love, Rachel? In order to get the big picture of Jacob's waiting period, we would like to use several verses from Genesis 29 (NIV). Rachel's father, "Laban said to him, just because you are a relative of mine, should you work for me for nothing? Tell me what your wages should be" (Verse 15). In verse 18, Jacob replied that he was in "love with Rachel and said, I'll work for you seven years in return for your younger daughter Rachel." Verse 20 tells us that Jacob, "served seven years to get Rachel, but they seemed like only a few days to him because of his love for her." Laban actually gave Leah, Rachel's sister, to Jacob instead, because it was custom to give the older daughter in marriage before the younger one. In return for another seven years of work, Jacob was finally given Rachel as his wife. His request was not answered the instant he desired Rachel. However, to Jacob, Rachel was worth waiting for.

Tomorrow may be the day that the Lord answers your request. Are you ready? The more difficult question is "are you ready if it is not tomorrow?" It may take time for your answer to be revealed because the timing is not right. If what you are praying over and seeking is from the Lord, it will be worth waiting for. God's plan is perfect and so is His timing. Will you trust Him as you wait?

Habakkuk 2:3, TLB, states, "But these things I plan won't happen right away. Slowly, steadily, surely, the time approaches when the vision will be fulfilled. If it seems slow, do not despair, for these things will surely come to pass. Just be patient! They will not be overdue a single day!"

Does God always have an answer?

Yes, God always has an answer. We promise you that He will never leave you hanging. He may answer you right away or He may take you through a period of waiting. He always answers, whether it is yes, no or wait. There will always be a reason for His timing and for His answer. You must trust Him. Pray and seek Him. Be still before Him. Listen to His still, small voice. Be patient and trust that your loving Father only has the best in store for your life.

PRAYER

Thank you Heavenly Father for always having an answer to our prayers. The answer may not always be what we were anticipating, but we know that You always hear our heart's cries and have a perfect plan for our lives. May You strengthen our walks with You when the answer is "no" or "wait." Help us to align our desires with Yours, for Your ways and Your timing is perfect.

In Jesus name,
Amen

VERSES

Genesis 29:15 (NIV): "Laban said to him, just because you are a relative of mine, should you work for me for nothing? Tell me what your wages should be."

Genesis 29:18 (NIV): "Jacob was in love with Rachel and said, I'll work for you seven years in return for your younger daughter Rachel."

Genesis 29:20 (NIV): "So Jacob served seven years to get Rachel, but they seemed like only a few days to him because of his love for her."

Habakkuk 2:3 (TLB): "But these things I plan won't happen right away. Slowly, steadily, surely, the time approaches when the vision will be fulfilled. If it seems slow, do not despair, for these things will surely come to pass. Just be patient! They will not be overdue a single day!"

Isaiah 40:31 (NIV): "but those who hope in (wait on) the Lord will renew their strength. They will soar on wings like eagles; they will run and not grow weary, they will walk and not be faint."

CHAPTER FIVE

WHEN IT SEEMS LIKE THE LORD IS NOT ANSWERING

The night before I (Heather) sat down to write this section for the book, the Lord impressed upon my husband's heart to read Psalm 13. He shared the words with me and wanted me to read them also. How appropriate for this section are the words of David as he wrote this Psalm. How amazing is the Lord we serve to lead my husband to read the very words that He longed for me to write as a part of this section. In order for us to better understand those times when you are unclear of the Lord's answer, let's dig deep into Psalm 13:1-6, NIV:

> *"How long, O Lord? Will you forget me forever? How long will You hide Your face from me? How long must I wrestle with my thoughts and every day have sorrow in my heart? How long will my enemy triumph over me? Look on me and answer, O Lord my God. Give light to my eyes, or I will sleep in death; my enemy will say, "I have overcome him," and my foes will rejoice when I fall. But I trust in Your unfailing love;*

*my heart rejoices in Your salvation. I will sing to the
Lord, For He has been good to me. "*

In the previous Psalm, David is crying out to the Lord in
despair. He asks the Lord "How long?" David is crying out
to God yet hears nothing. God is silent. God is not speaking.
He starts the Psalm with thoughts of the Lord forgetting him
forever. He says that there is sorrow in his heart and that he
is wrestling with his thoughts. To me, it sounds as if this
is a time of confession for David. He is in despair. He is
confessing to the Lord his sins, his past, his failures and is
asking the Lord to hear him and to forgive him. He is now
wrestling with the bad thoughts that once flooded his mind.
He is dealing with the sorrow that fills his heart over his past
mistakes.

He begs the Lord to hear him and answer him. He asks
that the Lord look upon him and give light to his eyes in
order that the enemy would not destroy him. Amidst the
despair, the anguish, the defeat, David is able to say the all
famous three letter word BUT. "But, I trust in your unfailing
love; my heart rejoices in your salvation. I will sing to the
Lord, for He has been good to me" (vs. 5-6). How reassuring
to know that regardless of the circumstances surrounding us,
the Lord will never take our salvation away from us. God's
love is unfailing. We may not hear Him but He is always near
because His love never fails us. Romans 8:38-39, NIV, tells
us that "neither death nor life, neither angels nor demons,
neither the present nor the future, nor any powers, neither
height nor depth, nor anything else in all creation, will be
able to separate us from the love of God that is in Christ
Jesus our Lord." He will never remove His love from us and
we can never be taken away from Him. Romans 8 solidifies
our relationship with Christ.

Why God is silent

Is He not there? Has He forgotten me forever? Is He not listening? Just like David, we may also go through periods when we ask the Lord "How long?" God was silent to David and He is also at times, silent toward us. Why would God be silent? You cry out to Him yet hear nothing. You search for His presence but feel that He is not there. You ask, seek and knock but feel as if the door isn't even going to budge. Why? "…How long will You hide Your face from me? (Psalm 13:1b, NIV).

We must rest assured that He is there. We all go through periods of silence from the Lord for various reasons. God always has a purpose and a plan and His ways are not always the same as ours (paraphrase of Isaiah 55:8-9, NIV). Nonetheless, His ways are always greater and His plan is always better.

Is there unconfessed sin?

Is there unconfessed sin in your life? Are you rebelling against God yet asking Him to hear you and answer your needs? Are you running far away from Him yet expecting Him to speak when you cry out to Him? Maybe He wants you to return to Him. Maybe He wants you to run home just like the parable of the lost son in Luke 15. Are you so far from God that you can no longer hear him? Maybe He is speaking but you are not listening. Come home. Confess. Repent and run into your loving Father's arms. He is waiting for you. He longs for you. He is being silent because He needs you to come home. Have you ever thought how God feels? Perhaps, He is thinking the same thing about you. Maybe He is wondering how long before you will return to Him.

If you feel that there is unconfessed sin in your life, don't despair. We serve a forgiving God. Pray the words of David in Psalm 51. This is a Psalm of David seeking forgiveness. David asks the Lord to wash and cleanse him, and to blot out his iniquities. In verse 10 he asks the Lord to "Create in me a pure heart, O God, and renew a steadfast spirit within me" (NIV). Does there need to be a time of confession in your heart? Sometimes the Lord is not answering us because He is waiting for us to come home.

Feel free to pray the following prayer or one of your own if you feel there is unconfessed sin in your heart.

Father of unfailing love,

I come to You broken. I come to You a sinner. I come asking for forgiveness. Forgive me for_____. Change my heart O God. Cleanse me. Wash me whiter than snow. I desire to be pure. I desire to be forgiven. I want to hear your voice but in order to be able to do so I must have my iniquities blotted out. Forgive me of my sins, Father. I am sorry that I have sinned against You. I want to come home. Thank You for never leaving me or forsaking me. Thank You for taking me back. Help me to remain strong when the devil prowls around like a roaring lion. May I put on the full armor of God and stay strong. Thank You that I am forgiven.

In the name of Jesus I pray,
Amen

Is He teaching you to be still?

We live in a very busy world. It seems that our days are getting shorter as well as the weeks, months and years. Life is passing us by like a whirlwind. At times it feels as if it is spinning out of control.

You just completed your MBA and you are busy climbing the executive ladder and all that the fast paced world of business offers. You work ten hour days five days a week and try to fit family, friends and errands into your weekend. You are a busy professional.

You are a mom and a wife who works full time. You go to work, come home, clean the house, cook dinner, get the children ready for bed, kiss the husband goodnight in order to wake up the next day and do it all over again. You are a busy woman.

You are a single man who works a part time job while studying for your Master's degree. In your spare time you lead a small group at church, play on your church's softball team and coach little league. You are a busy man.

Where has our time gone? When do we get to take a breather? When can we relax? It is no wonder we cannot hear God speak to us because we are too busy to sit still long enough to hear the Holy Spirit stir within our hearts. I (Heather) remember a time in college when the Lord had to get my attention because I was just too busy. That semester I was taking a full load of classes, including anatomy with lab. My week was packed before it even got started. I worked out in the morning before class. During the day I had classes and lab, while studying in between. On Monday nights, I led a girl's Bible study. I attended a campus ministry on Tuesday nights and helped lead worship. Leading worship also meant practice during the week. I went to church on Wednesday nights. Thursday nights I studied and then it was the weekend which was always crammed full. I was a busy college student. I was worn out and tired. Maybe half of my time was filled with ministry and fellowship, but I still had little time set aside for my *own* personal time alone with God.

Does that sound a little like you? Your week is filled up with ministry type tasks yet you lack the time you need to be alone and quiet with the God whom you are ministering for. During that period of my life I distinctly remember God being so quiet when I would pray and spend time with Him. I wasn't sure why He was so quiet. Spiritually I felt nothing. God was silent. I had no emotion whatsoever. I wasn't even able to cry. This feeling lasted for several weeks. Meanwhile, I kept on with my Bible studies, campus ministries and church. I was full of fellowship with other believers and with "doing" for the Lord, yet I lacked fellowship with my Lord. I missed Him. I longed to meet with Him and to feel His presence like I was used to. Where had He gone? Why was He so silent?

Finally, one night, alone in my room, a particular praise song came on the radio and my heart was filled with joy and my eyes filled with tears. In that very moment God spoke to me in such a way that I will never forget. In the same way He appeared to the priests in the Holy of Holies tent, He spoke to me. No, He didn't appear before me nor did I hear Him in an audible voice. However, He was present. The Lord was there with me in that room and I knew it. As tears rolled down my face, I felt the presence of the Lord as if His hands were on my back telling me to "slow down my child. You are going at such a fast pace that even I cannot get through to you." It was as if He were saying "You cannot hear Me because you are not being still enough to know that I am near." He was speaking to me from His words in Psalm 46:10 (NIV), "Be still, and know that I am God."

Can you relate? Do you feel the same way that I did that semester in college? It is good to do good works for the Lord but without a personal, daily walk with Him, our work is in vain. God may not be answering you because He wants you to be still. Get alone with God and listen for His voice. He wants to speak to you if you would only be still.

Is He teaching you a lesson through His silence?

I (Heather) sat in my big, brown, oversized, comfy chair to have my quiet time, when my oldest son was an infant. I couldn't help but notice him struggling to reach his teether that he had just moments before dropped under his bouncy seat. He whimpered just a little as he struggled to pick it up with all of his might. He almost got it but then dropped it once again. If only those tiny fingers were a little longer. He glanced at me, as if he was hoping that I would go over and help him like I always did. However, this time I decided to wait a little longer in order for him to figure out how to obtain the teether on his own. How would he ever learn to get toys himself if I helped him every single time? Eventually he would learn and figure it out. I have learned that at times I must step back and let him explore on his own. If he had not figured it out after a few tries, of course I would have lent a helping hand. However, in the meantime, he had to wait. During that time of waiting he was able to learn, grow and stretch his independence.

It seems as though our Heavenly Father looks down upon us as His children in the same way. We seek Him, we knock, yet at times we hear no answer. Why must we wait? Why must we have those periods in our lives when we do not hear His voice? We know He is near, yet we are not able to get a clear answer or direction over our prayers. Why must we wait? We need those times in our walk with the Lord when we must wait. It is during our time of waiting that we grow, learn and are more often than not, strengthened. Has the Lord ever led you through a period of waiting when you did not come out of it stronger than when you began your time of waiting?

If you are going through a waiting period, trust God through it. Though you may feel alone, you are not. Though you may not know the end result, God does. Even during your time of waiting, God has a plan. Use your God-ordained time of waiting to grow. Use this time for growth. Listen for what He is teaching you through His silence. It won't last forever. Trust Him in the middle of it and be a stronger person in the long run because of it.

PRAYER

Father, help us to hear Your voice when we feel You are not answering. We know that You always answer our prayers. Forgive us of our sins. Teach us to be still before You. May we learn through Your silence. We pray the same prayer of David from Psalm 13:5-6 "But, I trust in your unfailing love; my heart rejoices in your salvation. I will sing to the Lord, for He has been good to me."

In Jesus name,
Amen

VERSES

Romans 8:38-39 (NIV): "neither death nor life, neither angels nor demons, neither the present nor the future, nor any powers, neither height nor depth, nor anything else in all creation, will be able to separate us from the love of God that is in Christ Jesus our Lord."

Psalm 13:1b (NIV): "...How long will You hide Your face from me?"

Isaiah 55:8-9 (NIV): "For My thoughts are not your thoughts, neither are your ways My ways, as the heavens are higher than the earth, so are My ways higher than your ways and My thoughts than your thoughts."

Psalm 51:10 (NIV): "Create in me a pure heart, O God, and renew a steadfast spirit within me."

Psalm 46:10 (NIV): "Be still, and know that I am God."

Psalm 13:5-6 (NIV): "But, I trust in your unfailing love; my heart rejoices in your salvation. I will sing to the Lord, for He has been good to me."

PART TWO

OUR PRAYERS, OUR ANSWERS

We rejoice with you for completing the first section of our prayer book. We pray that you will allow the Lord to mold your prayer life through reading this section. May we glorify God through our transparency.

We desire to give you a glimpse of our personal prayer lives, as we share with you a variety of our prayer stories, journal entries and answers to our prayers. These were accumulated over a decade of praying together.

Going out on a Limb

I was recounting a story to Heather about a situation that I was in with another person who was becoming increasingly anxious and upset as a deadline we both had was approaching. The circumstances had not all been worked out, but I was not worried about it. I don't say that to sound arrogant or aloof, as I was well aware of the time crunch and I was doing everything I could from a human perspective. However, instead of worrying, I was praying about it and trusting in the Lord to work out all the details in His perfect timing, in His perfect way; which He did, at the last minute. In Isaiah 30:15, NKJV, He tells us, "...in quietness and confidence shall be your strength...."

As I told Heather about it, I made the comment, "Well, if anyone's going to hang out with me, they're going to have to go out on a limb." This means, having faith up until the last minute that God will work something out through prayer. You don't actually need something until the last minute, thus why fret about it in the meantime?

Out on the limb is where the good fruit is. It's not back at the trunk. It's out on the limb. Sure there's fruit along the way that may be good, but the best is at the end! Why settle for second best when you can push yourself a little further to have the very best? Yes, it takes more work to go out on the limb, than to climb the tree trunk. You must be careful that you don't lose your footing and that you have the end in sight. You must also have a safety net of people willing to catch you, lest you fall.

Hebrews 11:1, NKJV, states "Now faith is the substance of things hoped for, the evidence of things not seen." In fact, the entire chapter of Hebrews 11 speaks about men and women of faith in the Old Testament. Verse 6 goes on to say that God "...is a rewarder of those who diligently seek Him." Faith means not trusting the circumstances in front of you but trusting God with the outcome. Although you may not see a human answer, there is a God answer to situations. Habakkuk 2:4b, NKJV, states, "...the just shall live by faith."

We have and are continuing to learn not to worry. It is best to keep your eyes focused on the big picture and the end result. Let God handle all the details. He does a much better job of it than we do anyway.

Without a doubt, we've had our share of trials and tribulations. We've had our heart breaks, our losses and we've suffered through various crises and times of need. Yet, God has always been faithful to us. We continually hold out for the good stuff even though there may be ups and downs along the way. For over a decade we have prayed together. Through this we have learned through many of life's lessons that you *HAVE* to pray and hold out for the good stuff. The God stuff *is* the good stuff!

CHAPTER SIX

PRAYING FOR AND WITH OTHERS

This chapter is a great encourager to help you be mindful to pray for others when God lays it on your heart to do so and as an act of obedience to His word. Do not ignore the feeling you get when God brings someone to mind for you to pray for them. They may be in serious trouble and need help or some divine intervention. There is a reason why you are all of the sudden thinking about someone. Perhaps it is someone you've not seen or talked to in a very long time or perhaps it is someone you interact with on a regular basis. Regardless, stop what you are doing or thinking about and lift them up in prayer. No matter how long or short your prayer is, lift the other person up.

Likewise, one day, you will most likely be the one needing intercessory prayer. We can not begin to tell you how many times someone has come to either of us and said they felt like they needed to pray for us. How awesome is it when you yourself are unable to pray that God surrounds you with others to pray for your needs?! How much more awesome is it when others lift you up and don't know your circumstances yet somehow manage to pray about just whatever it is you are struggling with?

We are called to pray for others. Philippians 2:3-4, NKJV states, "Let each of you look not only for his own interests, but also for the interests of others." Praying for others include, loved ones, acquaintances, strangers and even our enemies. Yes, our enemies. In Matthew 5:44, NKJV, Jesus says, "...love your enemies, bless those who curse you, do good to those who hate you, and *pray* for those who spitefully use you and persecute you." We are called to pray for those people who hurt us. Even when Jesus was on the cross, He was still praying for others. In Luke 23:34, NKJV, He prayed, "..Father, forgive them, for they do not know what they do."

Family

> *"Honor your father and mother," which is the first commandment with promise: "that it may be well with you and you may live long on the earth (Ephesians 6:2-3, NKJV).*

Nothing is more important to either one of us than our families and relationships with them. We love them so much and would not be the women we are today without them. Throughout our times praying together, we have always included our families in our prayers.

We have continually come to the Lord on their behalf and prayed for them over situations that they may not even have been aware of. We have covered them in prayer over many of the needs in their lives. If one was sick, we prayed for healing. If another was having financial struggles, we prayed for provision. If anyone was hurting, we prayed for comfort.

We might not even realize the full scope of the impact of our prayers for them as we write this book. Yet they've been prayed for more fervently than any other single topic. We would strongly encourage you to pray for your loved ones as well. Prayer always makes an impact on others, whether you ever personally see that or not.

Heather and Kim

Praying for daddy

Following is an email that I sent out to family, friends and acquaintances on behalf of my daddy:

I just wanted to thank you all for your thoughts and prayers this week. It was definitely one of the most emotional weeks that I have ever had. It is weird to be on the other side of cancer. As most of you know I am a pediatric nurse for kids with cancer. I have worked with cancer patients for years now and must admit that this is not a side of cancer that I ever imagined facing. This past Monday daddy was diagnosed with stage III lung cancer.

He is having a brain MRI on Monday to make sure there is no sign of cancer there, and believing that the result is negative, he will start six weeks of radiation and chemotherapy the following week. Our family covets your prayers. I believe in the power of prayer, and would be so thankful if you desired to pass this prayer request to others.

Specifics:
1. Daddy's health and healing
2. Strength, decreased nausea and increased appetite (he already has these problems and hasn't even started chemo)
3. For a peace that surpasses all understanding!

From the bottom of our hearts, my family thanks you.

Blessings in Christ,
Heather

Thank you for allowing me to be so transparent and share a personal email of mine. It was a very difficult email to type, one that I never imagined having to type. Almost three months have passed since that particular email was sent and

I am typing the words to this book while my daddy is daily fighting his battle with cancer, which we recently found out has shrunk approximately sixty percent. He is trying his best to be strong and courageous but I know there are days when he just wants to give up. He is very weak, tired and is climbing a very difficult mountain. The good news is that the Lord is with him. I just mentioned to him the other day that he is in the Lord's hands and that either way, he will be okay.

I have never prayed for my dad more than I have done these past three months. My two boys fervently pray over Papa Joe and ask Jesus every night to heal his body and give him strength and energy. I have sent several more emails since the one you just read and I can almost hear the heart cries from people on my daddy's behalf. People that he has never even met have been on their knees for my dad. Prayer is such an amazing thing.

The mountains that we climb may be very difficult ones, but I know the Lord has a plan. I would not be able to walk alongside of my dad's battle with cancer without prayer.

Heather

Friends

"A mirror reflects a man's face, but what he is really like is shown by the kind of friends he chooses."
Proverbs 27:19, TLB

What a blessing friends are! Friends are incredible people God puts into your life to help add encouragement, provide shoulders for you to lean on, to be your road trip traveling buddies or for just plain fun.

But when I was thirteen years old, I did not feel like I had any friends at all. Perhaps that wasn't really the case. Or perhaps it was. However, when you are an adolescent, there are many different issues that you struggle with. Not having an abundance of friends may be one of them.

I remember the first lengthy prayer I ever prayed. No one really told me any specific "How To" of prayer. I remember laying there on my bed looking up at the ceiling and asking God to give me friends. I rambled on for thirty minutes and poured my heart out about how I wanted friends in my life. Well, lo and behold, you will never believe what happened the next day. Absolutely nothing. My prayer was not answered over night. For the next ten years or so, I didn't really think about that prayer again.

Fast forward to college. I transferred to the University of Georgia during the middle of the school year after having been at a community college. I knew my roommate and a handful of other people. However, UGA in the classic town of Athens, GA, was home and school to some 30,000 students. That can be a little overwhelming when you are just a face in the crowd.

This time I prayed not only for friends, but more specifically for godly, *Christian* friends. "The righteous should choose his friends carefully, for the way of the wicked leads them astray" (Proverbs 12:26, NKJV). I also prayed for an accountability partner. Proverbs 27:17 (NKJV) states, "As iron sharpens iron, so a man sharpens the countenance of his friend." I wanted to grow as a Christian so badly and I really wanted to be influenced by people with the same mind set.

Evidently God had the same desire for me. That next year He blessed me tremendously with some remarkable Christian friends. He put Christian friends in nearly all of my classes. These people were and continue to be incredible. The faith they had was what I wanted to experience myself. They talked about things, prayed about things and were focused on heaven above. You truly do become like the people you associate with and are influenced by. "Blessed is the man who walks not in the counsel of the ungodly, nor stands in the path of sinners, nor sits in the seat of the scornful; but his delight is in the law of the Lord, and in His law he meditates day and night. He shall be like a tree planted by the rivers of water, that bring forth its fruit in its season, whose leaf also shall not wither; and whatever he does shall prosper" (Psalm 1:1-3, NKJV).

God really planned that year out so intricately and wonderfully for me. Since they were in my classes, we also studied a lot together. It was during our study times, many conversations turned to that of faith and God. I was able to grow in my faith by the encouragement of others. The people who encouraged me the most and spur me onto the next level were surrounding me during college. Proverbs 11:14, NKJV states, "Where there is not counsel the people fall; but in the multitude of counselors there is safety."

One memorable example of the love of Christian friends was demonstrated to me during this time through my friend Tammy. I sprained my ankle at school, in one very embarrassing moment of not so graceful movements. My good friend and study partner at the time helped me up. He gave me a hand and made sure I was alright. That evening Tammy stopped over. She baked me some brownies and brought them over with a verse. "Two are better than one, because they have a good reward for their labor. For if they fall, one will lift up his companion. But woe to him who is alone when he falls, for he has no one to help him up" (Ecclesiastes 4:9-10, NKJV). Not only did I erupt in a fit of giggles at how perfect this verse was, but I also marveled that it was in the Bible! I thought what a perfect and fitting verse and it was meant just for me at that time!

I don't think that I will ever have to pray to have friends again in my lifetime. As Psalm 23:5, KJV states, "...my cup runneth over" with the blessings of godly friends! Since college, I've moved across the country, out of the country and done a lot of traveling in between. God has blessed me with friends all over the US and on different continents. I remember at one point thinking, "Where in the world did all of these people in my life come from?" And it was almost as if God smiled with and had a knowing look with a response of, "Well, you prayed for friends and I gave you friends."

Kim

Praying with others

There have been numerous times in my life that I have had the opportunity to get on my knees before our Father with others and pray. My earliest recollection was bedtime prayers with my mama. To this day, I am greatly encouraged by the memories of kneeling down beside my bed with her and my brother to pray before she tucked us in for the night.

The Lord has blessed me with a wonderful group of sisters in Christ. Some have been in my life for years and others only for a short time period. However, each of them encouraged me in the area of prayer. I loved praying with my roommates in college. The times of praying with my roommates are just too numerous to count. It was so encouraging to be able to have someone in your apartment to pray with over a matter right then and there.

During my sophomore/junior year of college, I had the opportunity to be a part of an "around the clock" prayer time with my church, Prince Avenue Baptist. The ideas was to have a member of the church pick a time slot to pray for an hour in order to have prayer covered twenty-fours, seven days a week. I was so blessed to have Mrs. Francis Harper pray the hour before me at one am and then call me at two am for my hour of prayer. She is the epiphany of a prayer warrior. I would never be the woman of prayer that I am today without having the honor to pray with her in the wee hour every Sunday morning.

One of my dearest friends, Emily and I started praying together for our families during college. It was awesome to have her pray on behalf of my family and vice versa. Several years after college, Emily and I had the blessing of having our little boys nine weeks apart. After having the boys, we began making weekly phone dates with each other to pray for our husbands and precious sons. As our families have grown, with the blessings of more children, we continue to pray for them and our husbands over the phone regularly. It fills my heart with joy to pray with her for our families.

God is good. He always places others in our lives to pray with. Our time alone with God to pray is very beneficial and necessary, but He also calls us to pray with others. Matthew 18:19-20, NIV, tells us that if "two of you on earth agree about anything you ask for, it will be done for you by my Father in Heaven. For where two or three come together in my name, there I am in the midst of them."

Heather

Blessings from God

Some of you may relate to this following answer to prayer. I still remember taking a walk with my good friend, Joy, from college when we started talking about her brother and sister-in-law and their desire to have a baby. I remember her asking me to pray for them. They were either having a hard time getting pregnant or would end up miscarrying. For many years, prayers were fervently lifted up on their behalf by many people. "The earnest prayer of a righteous man has great power and wonderful results" according to James 5:16b, KJV. They were such precious people and deserved nothing more than to have children of their very own. It was so hard to understand why the Lord kept making them wait. They tried for about seven years or so to get pregnant.

The Lord led them to seek out adoption and see where that route led them. Sometime later, they received the best news. There was a pregnant woman in town who desired to put her child up for adoption. She wanted this couple to be the parents of her baby! What a praise! I will never forget the day my friend told me the news. I still feel the joy in my heart when I even think of their longing to be parents and their answer to prayer. They became the proud parents of a wonderful little boy, and have since adopted another son into their family.

During this trial, were they ever hurt? Yes. Did they ever shed a tear or doubt God's reasoning? I am sure. But, were they faithful? Most assuredly, yes! Several or so years later, God answered their hearts cry. Maybe the journey was longer than they had desired and maybe things didn't turn out exactly how they would have planned it in their own human minds. But I guarantee you, they wouldn't trade the love and care they have for and are able to share with their precious sons for anything in the world. All along the Lord was working as they prayed and as others prayed. It just took time for these children who God designed just for them to come along. They and their sons are so happy and blessed.

The timing was just never right before. They had to keep their faith. They couldn't give up. They had to keep praying, keep believing and keep trusting in the awesome God they served. He is a God of big promises! Isaiah 55:8-9, NIV, "For My thoughts are not your thoughts, neither are your ways My ways," declares the Lord. "As the heavens are higher than the earth, so are My ways than your ways and My thoughts than your thoughts." How applicable is this verse to the above prayer. Did things go just as they had planned them? Did things happen as quickly as they expected? Maybe not, but how wonderful is the good news of God!? Yes, they may have had to wait, trust and pray fervently, but look at the end result. They are now the proud parents of two precious boys, who oh so greatly needed to one day be able to call them mommy and daddy. I am ever so happy for this couple and my heart greatly rejoices.

Psalm 127:3 (TLB): "Children are a gift from the Lord; they are His reward."

Heather

God's Healing Hand

Here is a copy of my journal entry from June 7, 1999:

I am so blessed to see God working in the lives of people I've prayed for. I ran into an old friend of mine on the night of May 15th. I talked to him for the first time in six years. I thought about him the next morning during church service and whether or not I should call him. It was more than a bit strange since I wasn't even in contact with him anymore. However, the thought kept persistently and stubbornly going through my head over and over and *over* again that *I needed to call him!* It was so persistent, that it was almost difficult to concentrate on the sermon. At the very end of the service, the church pastor and said, "If the Lord has laid it on your heart to call someone, you need to do it." I nearly fell out of the pew it shocked me so much that he said that!

I came home and debated all afternoon about what I should do. In the meantime, I went back to the evening worship. A different pastor had unknowingly prepared a sermon based on the same scripture we heard that morning. Those people who'd also been at the morning service chuckled a bit. Someone whispered to him that the same sermon had already been preached that morning. However, he was quite determined to preach the same text regardless.

I went home and called my friend at 10:30 that night. I didn't have a clue what to say. Thus, I said the only thing I knew to say. I told him I'd been praying for him. He immediately asked if it was because he'd broken his neck. He told me of a diving accident he'd been involved in two years prior. However, he'd recovered from it and was not paralyzed. I was shocked. I had *no idea* that he'd broken his neck. We continued to talk and reminisced for the next three hours.

After I got off the phone, I started thinking back. I began daily praying for him two years prior in January 1997. I remember I had a bad feeling about him back then. He'd broken his neck the same summer I had a bad feeling about him. However, I didn't know anything else to do at the time but pray.

The morning following our phone conversation, I opened my Bible. I still had my pen in my Bible marking the place where the same two sermons were preached the day before. Jesus sure didn't want me to miss the topic! It was Mark Chapter 2, Jesus healing and forgiving a paralyzed man. My friend didn't lose his life and was not paralyzed after breaking his neck. Wow. By medical standards, he could've easily died that day or if not at the very least been paralyzed from the neck down.

Mark 2:1-12 (NKJV) reads:

"And again He entered Capernaum after some days, and it was heard that He was in the house. Immediately many gathered together so that there was no longer room to receive them, not even near the door. And He preached the word to them. Then they came to Him, bringing a paralytic who was carried by four men. And when they could not come near Him because of the crowd, they uncovered the roof where He was. So when they had broken through, they let down the bed on which the paralytic was lying. When Jesus saw their faith, He said to the paralytic, 'Son, your sins are forgiven you.' And some of the scribes were sitting there and reasoning in their hearts. 'Why does this man speak blasphemies like this? Who can forgive sins but God alone?' But immediately, when Jesus perceived in His spirit that they reasoned thus within themselves, He said to them, 'Why do you reason about these things in your hearts? Which is easier, to say to the paralytic, "Your sins are forgiven to you"

or to say, "Arise, take up your bed and walk?" But that you may know that the Son of Man has power on earth to forgive sins" – He said to the paralytic, 'I say to you, arise, take up your bed, and go to your house.' Immediately he arose, took up the bed, and went out in the presence of them all, so that all were amazed and glorified God, saying, "We never saw anything like this!"

If you struggle with the reality of God, then ponder this question, how can I sit on my couch miles away and pray for someone without knowing what the circumstances are? Do you honestly think that it's mere coincidence that all of the above happened? Romans 8:26, NIV, states, "In the same way, the Spirit helps us in our weakness. We do not know what we ought to pray for, but the Spirit himself intercedes for us with groans that words cannot express. And he who searches our hearts knows the mind of the Spirit, because the Spirit intercedes for the saints in accordance with God's will."

Kim

Planting Flowers

*"For lo, the winter is past, the rain is over and gone.
The flowers appear on the earth..." Song of Solomon
2:11-12 NKJV.*

One year, when I lived in a little house by myself, I decided I wanted to plant some flowers. I wanted bright, yellow flowers, to indicate happiness and cheer. So I planted and watered some beautiful, little yellow flowers. Since I'm not really the green thumb type and had never had flowers before, I asked God to help the flowers grow. Short, sweet and quick prayer.

I watered the flowers initially, but then got busy with other things. Seldom and randomly, I remembered to water them, but not nearly enough. Then one day I came home from work. Much to my astonishment, the flowers were big and beautiful. I really couldn't understand it, as I'd not been caring for them as I should. Surely the flowers should be withered by now. There was really no way, humanly, that the flowers could've survived. Then I was instantly reminded that I prayed for the flowers to grow. Such a seemingly small prayer request, yet God hears every word we speak to Him.

It wasn't too long after this that Heather and I were talking. We were discussing the salvation of friends. I had a list of people that I regularly prayed for to come to know the Lord and have their own personal relationship with Him. I was feeling a bit stressed as I could not understand after all my praying, why most of these people had not come to know the Lord yet. The single most important thing to me is taking people to Heaven with me.

Heather then brought to my attention 1 Corinthians 3:6-7 (NKJV). Paul is speaking and states, "I planted and Apollos watered, but God gave the increase. So then neither he who plants is anything, nor he who waters, but God who gives the increase." I was instantly reminded of the flowers. I planted them. I (initially) watered them. But God is the only One who made them grow. Thus, I was quickly reminded that I had done and was doing what was asked of me. And that is to witness to and pray for others. The rest of it is in God's hands. It is God who changes people's hearts, but our prayers and encouragement that plant the seeds. "Keep on sowing your seed, for you never know which will grow - perhaps it all will" (Ecclesiastes 11:6, TLB).

Kim

Praying for the unsaved

The decision to accept Christ as my personal Lord and Savior was the best and most important decision that I have ever made. I will never forget the overwhelming feeling of peace that came over me the moment that ever so important decision was made.

As years from that decision day passed, I began to develop a desire for God to use me as a vessel to lead others to Christ. I wanted others to have the same peace that I felt when I accepted Christ as my Savior. I began to pray for the salvation of family members, friends and even those whom I did not know. Oh, if only all of creation would come to call upon the name of the Lord.

My prayers continued as well as my desire to be used by God to lead others to Him. During my freshman year of college, I attended a fall retreat with the college ministry at my church. Before the retreat our college pastor told us that a group of international students had been invited to join us at the retreat. An opportunity lay before us to be able to share the love of Jesus with those students who did not know Him as their Savior. My heart began to pound as the college pastor told us they were attending the retreat with us, for I knew the Lord was calling me to be an open vessel, ready and willing to be used by Him. He was calling me to begin to pray for the lost international students and to be open to what He had in store the following weekend at the retreat.

I did just that. I prayed. I sought the face of God and asked to be used by Him. I prayed, "Oh Lord, may I be the vessel used to draw an unsaved person to you. May I be used to add a new believer to your kingdom!" I hungered and thirsted to be used in such a capacity. The retreat came and I was ready. Use me Lord.

During one of the sessions, I just so "happened" to sit next to male and female international students. Their English was somewhat broken, so I helped interpret what the speaker was saying. After the session, the one student approached me and wanted me to explain a few more concepts that were mentioned in the Bible study. With a smile on my face an "Okay, God, I asked to be used by You, here we go" running through my head, I gladly explained the word of God to him. Through this time of learning, I was able to speak to him about Christ and salvation. By the end of our time talking, I was able to go over the plan of salvation with him and he is now our brother in Christ. Welcome to the kingdom. Praise Jesus. I was able to keep in touch with him several months after that and was able to help "spur him on" Hebrews 10:24 (NIV) states, "And let us consider how we may spur one another on towards love and good deeds." I encouraged him to begin reading his Bible daily, to start attending church and to surround himself with other believers.

As I write this section, my mind can't help but go back to that day. Oh Jesus, how I pray that this brother in Christ is still strong, still faithful and is still running hard after you. If he has strayed, oh Lord, I pray that You bring Your lost sheep home.

Heather

Never underestimate.....

Two friends of mine, Michael and Shane, were taking a trip to Florida. One of them was worried about the other's lifestyle and relationship with the Lord. The day they were traveling by car to Florida, I sat at my desk and lifted them up in prayer on and off for about three hours during a portion of their travel time.

Little did I know what impact this had. Once they returned, I found out that their conversation for the majority of the trip, specifically during the time I was praying, was about the Lord. It gave me goose bumps to hear that. To realize that a prayer you are praying for someone from miles away has such an instantaneous impact is a bit overwhelming. Particularly when that prayer is only between you and the Lord and no one else knows about it.

Never underestimate the impact you can have on others by lifting them up in prayer.

Kim

Russian Girls

Do crazy things ever happen to you? Do those random, crazy adventures ever pop up in your life unexpectedly? Do you ever cross paths with someone just for a brief moment and wonder if there was more reason to the crossing than just coincidence? I believe all of those situations are more than just mere coincidences. I think they are a God thing.

You know how you go and re-tell a story and afterwards you say "You just had to be there?" Well, that is the way I feel about the following story. I only hope you can picture the scene as you are reading it. The most unexpected event occurred when my friend Tammy came to visit my husband and I for the weekend. As a side note, I had just found out that I was pregnant and it was his birthday weekend. Tammy called to tell us she was at the gas station at our exit after getting really lost. Those of you reading this book who actually know her can only chuckle at that, right?

While she was waiting for us at the gas station, she ended up crossing paths with two Russian girls who were in the states for the year on a work pass. They were trying to get to Pigeon Forge, Tennessee where they were currently living. They had taken a little trip to Jamaica and had run out of money. A trucker brought them from the Atlanta airport to the gas station up from our house. My dear friend, Tammy wanted to help them out. She is a little more independent and daring than me. She thought maybe they could stay at our house over night and she could take them home the following morning. Being slightly less daring than she, my husband and I were a little hesitant. She told me to just wait until I got to the gas station and see just how precious they are. Well, they were absolutely precious and three and a half hours from their temporary home in Tennessee. They had planned on depending on various truck drivers to give them rides back to TN.

What were we to do? We didn't know these girls. However, we decided to take them up the highway a few exits because there would be more traffic there and more likely a better chance of getting a ride to Pigeon Forge. Well, to make a long story short, a few exits turned into many exits and before we knew it we passed the Georgia state line, Chattanooga, Knoxville and were well on our way to Pigeon Forge, Tennessee. We just kept driving and driving. It just seemed like the right thing to do. We drove three and a half hours dropped them off at their house and drove home. Mind you, Tammy had to drive the entire trip because my husband forgot his wallet with his drivers's license and not to mention we were both in our pajamas. Hey, don't laugh! We only thought we were going up the street to the gas station! We had no idea this would turn into an all night excursion. By morning it was my husband's birthday so the girls sang Happy Birthday to him in Russian.

I share this story with you because I wanted to bring home a point. The point being is this, we never know why our paths cross with certain people. To some, we may be the only Jesus others may see. Our conversations to these girls and our act of service could have impacted their lives forever. When the Lord places unexpected people in our paths we must trust that He has a plan. We have only had minimal contact with the girls through email from time to time since that day but our prayers for them may last an eternity. We can only pray that we were an example of Christ to our Russian girls.

Heather

Gas Station Trip

Heather came to visit me one weekend. When we got together, we made up our prayer lists and prayed together. Later on, for some reason, I began to feel a bit queasy. We drove to K-Mart to get some Sprite. We couldn't find the smaller, cold containers that can usually be located at the check-out line. Thus, we left and drove to the gas station just down the road.

As I walked in, there was a young man who was sitting on a stool. I got my drink and then went back out to the car. The young man came outside a few steps behind me.

Heather and I began talking to him. I remember at this point being doubled over in pain, while Heather went on to chat with him. I also remember clearly hearing the Lord in a not so audible voice saying, "This is nothing compared to what I went through." I also remember thinking of Paul and the pain he had, but that didn't stop him from witnessing to people. In 2 Corinthians 12:7-8, NKJV, Paul states, "...a thorn in the flesh was given to me."

As we went on to converse with him, he told us of how he was homeless and didn't have any food. An older lady approached as we were talking to him that was also friends with him. She herself was homeless. Heather and I talked to them for a bit and then left to go buy them dinner. We returned and sat with them for a bit longer. The guy asked me if I saw him looking at me as I walked into the store and told me the reason why was because he just *knew* there was a reason that I was there. We prayed with them before we left.

As we drove off, I noticed that the pain and queasy feeling I felt earlier were all gone. It seems as if the only reason for my pain was so we would get out of the house and encounter who God wanted us to encounter.

Kim

Gas Station Trip Take 2

I, too, want share the same story with you from my perspective. It is neat how we both remember the story in completely different ways. The Lord used both of us that night and taught both of us so much. Yet both of the lessons were so different. How amazing that the Lord can use the same incident and give us different perspectives of it.

I remember having a strong desire to witness to someone on the way to Kim's that evening. She and I prayed to have the opportunity to be used in the life of another person that night. God chose the man and woman at the gas station for exactly that. As Kim and I sat and chatted with this man we were able to share the good news of the Lord with him. Not only did we share Christ with him through words but by our actions. We gave him food. The Lord sent us there to meet his needs through food. Psalm 113: 7, NIV tells us that the Lord "raises the poor from the dust and lifts the needy from the ash heep; He seats them with princes, with the princes of their people." God uses us to take care of the poor and needy. We were called on that night to share God's word with this man, to pray with him and to give him food. Had we just walked right passed him, not stopping as the Lord drew us to this man, we would have missed out on the will of God and such a blessed night.

The female that we met was also homeless for the time being and was a Christian. She even gave me the name and address of her church in case I ever wanted to visit. I kept that piece of paper with me for years and prayed for this woman every time I came across it.

We may never cross either one of their paths again on this side of Heaven but I pray that both of them will be with us as we celebrate an eternity with our Savior. I do not know if the man ever accepted the Lord as his Savior but I pray the seeds that were planted that night will remain in his heart and he will call upon the name of the Lord.

Don't let a day pass you by without allowing the Lord to use you in the life of those He places in your path. The woman at the checkout counter, the teller at the bank, your child's teacher, the homeless guy on the street corner, and the list goes on and on, but you may be the only Jesus they ever see. Don't let the opportunity to be used pass you by.

Heather

Hummer Time

It was Labor Day weekend 2004 and I was in Florida on a big singles church retreat at the beach with North Point Community Church from Alpharetta, GA. Hurricane Frances was quickly approaching. It crossed southern Florida and was quickly approaching the panhandle where our retreat was. After some discussion amongst the organizers, they decided to evacuate us and thus end the retreat a day early.

I stood watching the news about the devastation that had just hit our neighbors to the south. There was a news reporter interviewing a man about what he'd just lost. He spoke of how he owned a gym on the beach and that it was now all gone. I can only imagine what a wonderful gym it was. He spoke of how he arranged the equipment so people could look out over the ocean while they exercised. How amazing it must have been to see the beauty of God's creation everyday while also working toward greater health. His eyes filled with tears and his voice quivered as he also recounted about how his father had just passed away only two months before. The man went on to say that all he had left was his hummer and his dog. He stated he'd been sleeping in it for the last few nights since the storm.

My heart went out to him as I saw the pain he was experiencing. I quickly said a prayer for him right then. But I also asked God to remind me to pray for him every time I saw a hummer. Wouldn't you know that I saw more hummers on the road over the next few weeks than I'd ever seen in my life? God must've known this man needed some prayer during that time. I faithfully prayed for him and his needs every time I saw a hummer. I don't know his name and I don't know anything more about him than that. However, I know that God stirred my heart to pray for him.

Kim

Teaching

My good friend Becki had just completed her teaching certificate and was applying for a new job. She had been applying and interviewing, yet nothing had turned up and the school year was about to begin.

She phoned me to ask if I could pray for her. It was Thursday and she had an interview on Friday. School started on Monday. If she didn't get this job, then she'd likely have to wait an entire school year before being able to teach since most contracts for teaching had already been filled for the year.

I reminded her of the verse in Matthew 21:22 (NKJV), "And whatever things you ask in prayer, believing, you will receive." I told her that she needed to *believe* she already had the job. But in the meantime, I told her I would believe for her. Heather and I immediately prayed for her after our phone conversation.

She phoned the next day to say she'd gotten the job.

Kim

Working 9 to 5

Work. Well, it's called that for a reason. Otherwise, we'd call it play. I remember during my first real job, I would listen to Mary Welchel's radio broadcast "The Christian Working Woman" every morning while I was getting ready. It was so encouraging and always provided me with insight into potential work situations.

One of her programs discussed starting a prayer group at work. Although I thought this was a wonderful idea and wanted to do this, I wasn't really sure how to go about it. It was definitely outside of my own personal comfort zone to begin this group. However, it was also most definitely a God thing. I was reminded of hearing Dr. Henry Blackaby, speak while I was in college. He is the author of the Bible study, "Experiencing God." He made one profound statement that has always stuck with me. He stated that "You may be the *only* one called to do something for the Lord and if you don't do it, then no one else will either."

Regardless of how far outside of my comfort zone this work prayer group was, I initiated it. I began talking to my colleague who sat in the cubicle next to me about it. Come to find out she was also a believer. During our fifteen minute breaks she and I would go and sit at the picnic tables outside to lift each other up in prayer. Slowly, one by one, others started to join us. Within a few short weeks time, nearly half of the company would join us outside as we led a prayer group everyday. It was really a bit mind boggling to me. I never fathomed that it could happen just as Mary discussed. Sure enough though, it did.

Many of the people who joined us were in desperate need of prayer and encouragement. In Matthew 9:37 (NKJV), Jesus said to His disciples, "...the harvest truly is plentiful, but the laborers are few." I realized the needs of my coworkers spanned further than I'd ever imagined. Amazing things happened as a result of our faithfulness to pray.

Kim

Psalm 139

I was born with clubbed feet which required two surgeries as a child. On my dad's side of the family, the second and third child for five generations, were born with either crippled hands or feet. I was born into the fourth generation. When I found out that I was pregnant with my second child, I began to worry that this baby would have a deformity of some sort. My husband and I began praying for the Lord to remove this "generational bondage" from our child because he would be my second child and was the fifth generation. We decided to claim Psalm 139:14a, NIV, "I praise you for I am fearfully and wonderfully made." Prior to claiming this scripture, I was filled with stress and worried constantly about the precious child in my womb. This verse helped me so much. Peace flooded my soul after I decided to turn this prayer request over to the Lord and believe in His word. I want to share with you three of my personal prayers that I wrote in my Bible beside that verse.

July 2006: Oh Lord, we claim this verse for our precious Jacob. May his fingers, hands, toes and feet all form perfectly without any problems whatsoever. We claim Your word for his body formation.

The next month we went for our ultrasound and I added the following prayer.

August 2006: Praise God. Dr. Nathan saw no malformation on the ultrasound. Glory to God. We continue to pray for good news.

Jacob was born and the following prayer was added:

November 19, 2006: Praise God! Jacob Avery is fearfully and wonderfully made. His hands, toes and feet are perfect.

Not only was Jacob born without any hand or feet deformities, our third baby, Emma Rose also has perfect hands and feet. It was an absolute miracle from the Lord to my family. We serve an amazing God. He is the ultimate physician and healer.

Heather

PRAYER

God please help me to be aware of the needs of others, whether I know the person or not. Please take the blinders off my eyes so that I can be of help to someone. If I can help in a tangible way, help me to know that.

The moment You lay upon my heart to pray for someone, may I do so that very instant. I may not speak with beautiful words, but just lifting their name up in prayer is enough for the Holy Spirit to interpret my requests before you, Heavenly Father. We know that when we are faithful to pray, You are faithful to hear our cries and answer them. May we always be mindful to pray for others.

Father, I come before you right now on behalf of (_____ ____) and I pray for them right now regarding (_____.) I thank you Father, in advance, for all You are going to do as a result of the prayers lifted up on their behalf.

In Jesus name,
Amen

VERSES

Isaiah 30:15 (NKJV): "...in quietness and confidence shall be your strength...."

Hebrews 11:1 (NKJV): "Now faith is the substance of things hoped for, the evidence of things not seen."

Hebrews 11:6 (NKJV): God "...is a rewarder of those who diligently seek Him"

Habakkuk 2:4b (NKJV): "...the just shall live by faith."

Matthew 5:44 (NKJV): "...love your enemies, bless those who curse you, do good to those who hate you, and *pray* for those who spitefully use you and persecute you."

Luke 23:34 (NKJV): "..Father, forgive them, for they do not know what they do."

Ephesians 6:2-3 (NKJV): "Honor your father and mother," which is the first commandment with promise: "that it may be well with you and you may live long on the earth."

Proverbs 27:19 (TLB): "A mirror reflects a man's face, but what he is really like is shown by the kind of friends he chooses."

Proverbs 12:26 (NKJV): "The righteous should choose his friends carefully, for the way of the wicked leads them astray."

Proverbs 27:17 (NKJV): "As iron sharpens iron, so a man sharpens the countenance of his friend."

Psalm 1:1-3 (NKJV): "Blessed is the man who walks not in the counsel of the ungodly, nor stands in the path of sinners, nor sits in the seat of the scornful; but his delight is in the law of the Lord, and in His law he meditates day and night. He shall be like a tree planted by the rivers of water, that bring forth its fruit in its season, whose leaf also shall not wither; and whatever he does shall prosper."

Proverbs 11:14 (NKJV): "Where there is not counsel the people fall; but in the multitude of counselors there is safety."

Ecclesiastes 4:9-10 (NKJV): "Two are better than one, because they have a good reward for their labor. For if they fall, one will lift up his companion. But woe to him who is alone when he falls, for he has no one to help him up."

Psalm 23:5 (KJV): "...my cup runneth over"

Matthew 18:19 (NIV): "...if two of you on earth agree about anything you ask for, it will be done for you by my Father in Heaven."

Matthew 18:20 (NKJV): "For where two or three come together in my name, there I am in the midst of them."

James 5:16b (KJV): "...the earnest prayer of a righteous man has great power and wonderful results."

Isaiah 55:8-9 (NIV): "For My thoughts are not your thoughts, neither are your ways My ways," declares the Lord. "As the heavens are higher than the earth, so are My ways than your ways and My thoughts than your thoughts."

Psalm 127:3 (TLB): "Children are a gift from the Lord; they are his reward."

Romans 8:26 (NIV): "In the same way, the Spirit helps us in our weakness. We do not know what we ought to pray for, but the Spirit himself intercedes for us with groans that words cannot express. And he who searches our hearts knows the mind of the Spirit, because the Spirit intercedes for the saints in accordance with God's will."

Song of Solomon 2:11-12 (NKJV): "For lo, the winter is past, the rain is over and gone. The flowers appear on the earth..."

1 Corinthians 3:6-7 (NKJV): "I planted and Apollos watered, but God gave the increase. So then neither he who plants is anything, nor he who waters, but God who gives the increase."

Ecclesiastes 11:6 (TLB): "Keep on sowing your seed, for you never know which will grow - perhaps it all will."

Hebrews 10:24 (NIV): "And let us consider how we may spur one another on towards love and good deeds."

2 Corinthians 12:7-8 (NKJV): "...a thorn in the flesh was given to me."

Psalm 113:7 (NIV): "raises the poor from the dust and lifts the needy from the ash heep; He seats them with princes, with the princes of their people."

Matthew 21:22 (NKJV): "And whatever things you ask in prayer, believing, you will receive."

Matthew 9:37 (NKJV): "...the harvest truly is plentiful, but the laborers are few."

CHAPTER SEVEN

SCHOOL AND CAREER

In addition to the decisions of salvation, marriage and children, we can probably agree that decisions about school and career are also high on the list for life decisions. You are probably asked, beginning in elementary school, what you want to be when you grow up. It is a big decision to have to begin to think about at such an early age. You aren't even sure at that point if you like vegetables or no. You are still trying to decide which super hero or princess is your favorite.

Big decisions have to be made when you come to the point of deciding which college to attend, whether or not you should choose to go to college at all and your career decision. We cannot even fathom making those decisions alone. For us as Christians, we are not alone. The Lord tells us He will never leave us nor forsake us (Deuteronomy 31:6b, NKJV). How reassuring to lean on the Lord for such a major decision. It would be much easier to make such big decisions if only we would give God our all and trust Him to lead and guide our steps.

The book of Proverbs is called the book of wisdom. If you are trying to make a big decision and are seeking the Lord, then you should lean upon His word and seek what

He has to say from Proverbs. Why, in the very first chapter, He tells us in verse 5 to "let the wise listen and add to their learning, and let the discerning get guidance" (NIV). Lean on the words from Proverbs 3:5-6 (NIV), "Trust in the Lord with all your heart and lean not on your own understanding; in all your ways acknowledge Him, and He will make your paths straight." Oh how good is the wisdom of the Lord when you have an important decision to make, such as which school to attend or which career path to take.

Praying in the park

I always had a "for sure" answer when I was asked what I wanted to be when I grew up. Without a doubt, a pediatrician! As mentioned in Chapter Six, I was born with a clubbed foot and hospitalized several times as a child. As a result of those experiences, I wanted to be a pediatrician. I was also very touched by St Judes' telethons that I used to watch when they raised money for the children's research hospital in Memphis, Tennessee for children with cancer. For these reasons, I started out my freshmen year at the University of Georgia as pre-med. I was going to be a doctor.

After my first quarter of college, I felt the Lord beginning to stir my heart about my career choice. What? Do you not want me to become a doctor, Lord? But that is what I've always wanted to be. This led me to become uncertain if what I wanted and what the Lord wanted for my future were the same thing. It weighed heavily on my heart.

I prayed over my declared major for several weeks but had no clarity whatsoever. The end of the quarter was soon coming to an end and I needed to make a decision in order to register for classes. My heart was heavy and I was very uncertain over what to do. I had no clear direction from the Lord. At church one night, my friend Amy, spoke of going to the park and praying over a major life decision. I decided that the next day I would do just that. Rain or shine, I was taking my journal, pen and Bible to the park to have some alone time with God, until He revealed His plan to me. I no longer wanted to go along with "Heather's plan" for my life, but "God's plan" for my life. Jeremiah 29:11 (NIV) "For I know the plans I have for you, declares the Lord, plans to prosper you and not the harm you, plans to give you hope and a future."

Speaking of rain or shine, there was no raincheck on my day alone with God. That morning, the sky was filled with dark clouds and rain soon began to fall from the sky. Thus, the pouring rain would just have to be a part of my day. Maybe it would mean that I wouldn't be able to sit on a blanket by the lake like I usually did, however I was determined to have my alone time with God. The rain made it so that the park was completely empty. It was as if it were me and God, all alone.

I sat alone in my car and remember throwing my watch down on the floorboard of my car. I wasn't on a time table and I wasn't planning on leaving until the Lord told me His desire for my future. I even prayed that. I prayed, "Lord, I am not concerned with time. My watch is on the floor. I am not planning on leaving here until I know that You and I are on the same page." Of course, along with that prayer, I had hoped the Lord would reveal Himself to me before dark. After several hours of praying and journaling, praying and journaling, and more praying and journaling, I had an overwhelming sense of peace that I was not to continue on the track to practice medicine in the anticipation of becoming a physician. After weighing the pros and cons, the Lord revealed to me that the financial benefit and prestige of becoming a physician did not outweigh my strong desire to marry and one day have children. He gave me the desire to be able to stay at home with my children without having to work long hours.

There is nothing wrong with those of you reading this book who are physicians. In fact, one of my very best friends is a physician. She, too, desires to marry and raise children. However, that was not how the Lord desired for me to use my time. Instead, four and a half years later, He allowed me to graduate with a bachelors of science in nursing. Believe it or not, I am working with children who have cancer. It is the best job ever. I love it and my life has been forever changed by the awesome children and families that have impacted my life. Along with that, I work twelve hour shifts only twice a week so I am able to spend the majority of my week at home with my children.

I hope this has encouraged some of you if you are struggling with a decision that needs to be made. May you walk away with the following in mind. You need to make sure that you are on the path the Lord has for you and not your own. I can't even imagine how different the past ten years of my life would have turned out had I not been obedient to the Lord and instead went along with my own desire for the future by remaining a pre-med major. Listen to the Lord. Be quiet and still before Him. 1 Kings 19:12b NKJV states that the Lord spoke in "a still small voice." He is speaking, but you must listen in order to hear Him. Take some time just for you and God. I am not telling you to sit in the rain like I did, but get away and get to God! Maybe He's speaking to you now, do you hear Him?

Heather

Where to attend Nursing School

I loved my years at the University of Georgia. It was the best years of my life, aside from now being married and being a mommy, of course. It was a time of growing and learning who I was as well as a time to make life long friendships. I will cherish those years in my heart forever. However, UGA did not have a nursing program. I hated the thought of leaving the classic town of Athens, GA. However, I knew in order to go to nursing school leaving would soon become a reality. I might have left kicking and screaming, okay actually crying and wiping away tears, but sooner or later I knew I had to move away to nursing school. But where? Where would the Lord lead me from UGA? Where would my path in life take me next?

After much prayer, I decided to apply to the Medical College of Georgia in Augusta and as a back up, Clayton College and State University. I really wanted to go to MCG but applied to CCSU because that was in my hometown and I would be able to move back in with my parents in order to save a little money. Again, let me reiterate, I really, *really* wanted to go to MCG. I had a few friends there and a few more would be coming in the next few years. Besides, who wanted to move back home and go to a local college when they had already moved out and been on their own for a few years? Not that mama's home cooking wasn't a bonus!

I remember the day that the letter came accepting me to MCG! Hooray!! I got in! I got in! I was ecstatic. If I had to leave UGA, then my next pick would be to go to MCG. Thank you Jesus for my acceptance letter. "Not so fast, dear one" spoke the Lord to my heart. "I have a different plan for you." "For my thoughts are not your thoughts, neither are your ways My ways, declares the Lord. As the heavens are higher than the earth, so are My ways than your ways and My thoughts than your thoughts" (Isaiah 55:8-9, NIV). Even though I had been accepted to my school of choice, the Lord began to stir in my heart that He wanted me to move home and go to Clayton State. And of course that acceptance letter also came in the mail. Are you sure God? I might have a little wax in my ear and maybe I am not hearing you correctly. Well, I did hear Him correctly. He spoke very clearly to my heart and I knew I could either be obedient and follow Him or do my own thing and face the consequences. I have learned that it is best to follow the Lord's lead. Thus, I packed my things and moved back home to attend Clayton College and State University.

Prior to moving, the last church service that I attended, the Lord allowed the choir and praise team to play two of my favorite praise songs at that time, "As the Deer" and "Shout to the Lord." As tears ran down my cheeks, I knew the Lord did that just for me. He knows me so well. After all, He did create me. He knew my favorite praise songs and that was His way of telling me everything was going to be okay and that I had to trust Him. I had to follow long and hard after Him, even when His desires were not exactly the same as mine.

As I sat to write this section, I ran across a little note that a dear friend placed in my Bible during my very last church service while I was still in Athens. Before I tell you the words to her note, I must add that God is so good. The sweet words of my friend, jotted down on a church tithing envelope were as follows, "I was praying for you even as he sang. I found this verse this morning. It's yours. 'Do not grieve, for the joy of the Lord is your strength.' Nehemiah 8:10b (NIV)." What a perfect verse. And what a perfect last church service.

I may never know all the reasons, this side of heaven, for the Lord leading me back home, but I have a few thoughts in my mind as to why. My family faced several trials and tribulations that year, with one being my dad suffering from an illness, prior to his recent diagnosis of cancer. I needed to be there to help take care of my family. It was tough at times but I know I was only strengthened as a result of it. I met some really neat people in nursing school and I know that the rest of my life has been mapped out the way it has as a result of my being obedient to my Heavenly Father's calling.

Heather

Getting Into Graduate School 2001

I had been researching colleges for graduate school. I must admit that I really love to travel and thus was looking at colleges all over the country. One of my choices was Colorado State University.

It just so turned out that my parents were taking a vacation to Colorado that summer. I asked if they could stop by and check out the campus for me while they were out that way to see what they thought. Upon returning in July, they proceeded to tell me that there were still spots available (even though I wasn't planning on going for another year) and that the school would love for me to come that year.

Thus, in about three and a half weeks time, I applied to graduate school, got accepted and moved across the country. I moved there with no security of financial aid, no place to live, no car and not knowing anyone. I took the GRE on a Thursday morning and flew out to Colorado that afternoon, to start school the next day. Talk about having to have faith in God! My acceptance was contingent on my scores!

I literally went out there on a wing and a prayer. However, I truly believed it was a "God thing" for me to go. Although there was a lot to do in a short period of time, when God says "Go" then you go and let Him handle the details. Within two to three days, I had a place to live, I had transportation and I had met some wonderful people. One of my friends from class, Nicole, generously offered to drive me to the store so I could buy a bike. She showed me around town and made me feel welcome. Had I tried to do all this on my own without prayers, it surely would've been a disaster. God truly worked out every single detail, far beyond what I could have ever imagined! All with perfect timing!

Sometimes, God works swiftly in our life plans and at other times, it may seem like things are never going to happen or work out. However, no matter how long or short you have to wait for prayers to be answered, know that above all if you wait on God, the timing is perfect. If He says "Go" then go, if He says, "Wait" then wait. "Rest in the Lord, and wait patiently for Him..." Psalm 37:7 NKJV.

Above all, trust Him; trust Him with the details. He knows your needs. He also knows your wants and desires. After all, He did create you. "Trust in the Lord with all your heart, and lean not on your own understanding; in all your ways acknowledge Him, and He shall direct your paths" Proverbs 3:5-6, NKJV.

Kim

Completing Graduate School - Stay or Go?

After all this talk about school and education, can you believe that I had struggles with the graduate degree I'd chosen? I truly do believe that it was in God's plan for me to move across the country and attend graduate school. However, I felt quite unsettled about the profession I was studying to be a part of and never really felt it was a good fit for me. I struggled with this during my entire first year.

That summer, I spent in a great deal of time praying regarding whether or not to return and complete the last year of the program. I felt as if I were at a crossroads and didn't know which way to go. I continued to pray all the way up until the drop date for Fall semester.

It was the day before I had to decide what to do. I drove up to Breckenridge, Colorado to pray and read my Bible. Heather read some verses to me the night before. Even though she was really amazed at how they related to me, I wasn't at the time. It was late and I was tired, thus what she read didn't really register with me.

I had decided to pray and read until I had an answer regarding what to do, no matter how long it took. I was very inspired to do this, as Heather had shared with me her "Praying in the Park" story years before while we were still undergrads. Now I felt I needed to do the same in order to know which direction to go.

The afternoon I arrived in Breckenridge, I re-read the same verses Heather had read to me: 2 Corinthians 8:10-11, NKJV, "And in this I give advice: It is to your *advantage* not only to be doing what you began and were desiring to do a *year* ago; but now you also must *complete* the doing of it; that as there was a readiness to desire it, so there also may be a completion out of what you have."

Whoa! God was pretty direct. It gave me goose bumps to read those verses. I didn't even know those verses were in the Bible. Initially, I thought God would lead me to some sort of analogous story relating to my events and be able to tie it in somehow. However, God knows that sometimes I can be a little thick-headed and need a very direct answer.

God also has a sense of humor. I read those verses first thing when I got up there. It wasn't too long after that, at the altitude of some 10,000 feet, that I began to experience all those symptoms that go along with altitude sickness. I got dizzy, light-headed and short of breath. I thought to myself, "Well, I'm glad He gave me an answer right away so I can drive back down the mountain to a more oxygen-rich environment"

In all seriousness though, I do recommend that if you are struggling with a big decision that you find a place of solitude to go and pray about it. If you live near mountains, go to the top. There's just something symbolic about going up in height to talk to God. "Now it shall come to pass in the latter days that the mountain of the Lord's house shall be established on the top of the mountains, and shall be exalted above the hills; and all nations shall flow to it. Many people shall come and say, 'Come and let us go up to the mountain of the Lord, to the house of the God of Jacob; He will teach us His ways, and we shall walk in His paths'...." (Isaiah 2:2-3 NKJV).

There was a quote that I ran across while I was in school. It was from Corrie Ten Boom, a wonderful and encouraging person who was held captive in Ravensbruck Concentration Camp. After her release from there, she began a ministry, sharing the love of Christ. One of her quotes that hit home with me was that, "Every experience God gives us, every person He puts in our lives, is the perfect preparation for the future that only He can see."

I held onto this quote and the verses mentioned during my final year of the program. I lived in International student housing, as one of the few Americans during that year. I loved every minute of it. I loved being around all the different ethnicities. I loved meeting the people, learning the customs, the languages and everything about them. I continue to keep in contact with many of these people who've since returned home to their countries.

I realized that my time there was not for mere academics, but for life education. We have what we consider "detours" in life for many different reasons. We may discover why one day or we may not. But, as my mother told me while I was in school, "Not everything is about you." She couldn't have been more right. Perhaps the only reason I was given the opportunity to go was to be an encouragement to someone else and to reach out to them with the love that Christ would.

Kim

Jobs

I was trying to decide about taking a certain job. I didn't know whether or not to accept the position I had been offered. I prayed about it. I phoned my new potential employer to discuss some possible concerns I had. Her response was very positive to all my concerns. Thus I decided to take the position. I had a complete peace about it.

My friend, Brad, in Colorado sent me an email not too long after I accepted this position. He told me that he had been praying for me on his way to work that morning. In the email, he said, "I just felt like I should pray for you and I lifted you up and asked that God would give you wisdom, discernment in your decisions and a peace about them." He also stated that having a peace about something is "one of the ways that you know what you are doing is right." Furthermore, he was praying for me just prior to my phoning my new employer and taking the position. With the time difference, he was praying at close to 7 AM (9 AM my time.) I took the position at 9:30 my time.

What can I say? Prayer works. Right when you need it. Thus, if the Lord lays it on your heart to pray for someone, please be mindful of it. It is important to pray for someone when the Lord brings it to your mind. You never know what someone may be going through and your prayers may be just what is needed to help them out.

Kim

PRAYER

Dear Heavenly Father,

I come before You to ask that You guide and lead my career direction and path. I ask that You be a part of every decision I make and put my feet on the right path. Help me to always keep in mind what the end result is of every career decision I make and not merely focus on the immediate gratification. Help me to know that You've given me certain gifts, talents and abilities to use to glorify You in my career.

Lord, I ask that You open my eyes to new possibilities and make me aware of opportunities where I would be most happy and use my gifts most effectively in my job. I pray that You will help me to remember that not everything in life is about me.

In Jesus name,
Amen

VERSES

Deuteronomy 31:6b (NKJV): "He will not leave you nor forsake you."

Proverbs 1:5 (NIV): "Let the wise listen and add to their learning, and let the discerning get guidance."

Proverbs 3:5-6 (NIV): "Trust in the Lord with all your heart and lean not on your own understanding; in all your ways acknowledge Him and He will make your paths straight."

Jeremiah 29:11(NIV): "For I know the plans I have for you," declares the Lord, "plans to prosper you and not to harm you, plans to give you hope and a future."

1 Kings 19:12b (NKJV): "a still small voice."

Isaiah 55:8-9 (NIV): "For my thoughts are not your thoughts, neither are your ways my ways, declares the Lord. As the heavens are higher than the earth, so are my ways than your ways and my thoughts than your thoughts."

Nehemiah 8:10b (NIV): "...for the joy of the Lord is your strength."

Psalm 37:7 (NKJV): "Rest in the Lord, and wait patiently for Him..."

2 Corinthians 8:10-11 (NKJV): "And in this I give advice: It is to your *advantage* not only to be doing what you began and were desiring to do a *year* ago; but now you also must *complete* the doing of it; that as there was a readiness to desire it, so there also may be a completion out of what you have."

Isaiah 2:2-3 (NKJV): "Now it shall come to pass in the latter days that the mountain of the Lord's house shall be established on top of the mountains, and shall be exalted above the hills; and all nations shall flow to it. Many people shall come and say, 'Come, and let us go up to the mountain of the Lord, to the house of the God of Jacob; He will teach us His ways, and we shall walk in His paths.' For out of

Zion shall go forth the law, and the word of the Lord from Jerusalem."

1 Corinthians 2:16 (NIV): "For who has known the mind of the Lord, that he may instruct him, but we have the mind of Christ."

Ephesians 1:17-18 (NIV): "I keep asking that the God of our Lord Jesus Christ, the glorious Father, may give you the Spirit of wisdom and revelation, so that you may know Him better."

CHAPTER EIGHT

FINANCES

How many of you reading this have ever had to rely on the Lord financially? If so, we believe it can be a very trusting time in your spiritual life. The amazing thing about it, though, is that we know that the Lord will come through and meet our needs according to His precious will. How do we know that, you ask? We know that because He promises it in His word. He tells us in Philippians 4:19, NKJV that "God shall supply all your needs according to His riches in glory by Christ Jesus." He promises to take care of the birds of the air and animals of the land, will He not even more so take care of His people? (Matthew 6:25-34, NKJV). He chose us and loved us so much that He gave up His very Son so that we may have life. We don't think He would do that to leave us in need.

Trusting God financially is often a hard concept to grasp because there are individuals out there who have never and will never hurt financially. Then there are those who can never seem to get ahead and never will. Our focus in this section is not necessarily on either of those extremes but simply trusting God and praying for the daily needs in our lives and knowing that Lord will meet our needs when we seek Him.

Money, wealth and a hearty fortune are things society tells you to seek after to be considered successful. In this section, we want to share some of our own financial struggles and triumphs with you, as well as sharing what scripture tells us about money and finances. We don't claim to be experts in the field of finance. We can't give you a breakdown of how to spend your money. Stocks, bonds, savings, retirement, investments and so on are a little out of our realm of expertise. (We would recommend seeking out a Christian financial advisor if this is something you need detailed assistance with.) What we can do is share with you verses from God's word and stories of how God has provided for us financially.

Getting a Car

Don't you just love how much a car costs these days? New or used. Makes no difference. They are still pricey. A number of years ago, I was driving an older model car. Some of my friends kindly referred to it as the "boat." Okay, okay, so it really was a bit long and large. However, my dad had gotten a really good deal on it and it was in excellent condition. It lasted me through college and for a few years after. However, I knew it was not destined to last forever, no matter how well it was maintained.

During the mornings, I would listen to Larry Burkett on the radio. He was founder of Christian Financial Concepts, now known as Crown Financial Ministries. He had a short, yet, powerful radio broadcast airing every morning regarding God's principles on money. I remembered hearing him say over and over again, not to buy a new car. It depreciates as soon as it is driven off the lot. You lose money on this investment. He strongly encouraged people to buy used cars that were affordable and maintain them. He encouraged people not to take out a car loan for a car because "...the borrower is servant to the lender" (Proverbs 22:7 NKJV). He told his listeners that rather than worry about how your are going to afford a car, pray about it and trust God to meet this need. "Be anxious for nothing, but in everything by prayer and supplication, with thanksgiving, let your requests be made known to God" (Philippians 4:6 NKJV).

Thus I started specifically praying for a car, before I needed one. I knew that I did not have the money to buy a car. I prayed for a car that was $2,000, with less than 50,000 miles and that was a four-door because that car insurance was cheaper than a two-door. You may be thinking to yourself, "A car with that low of mileage and for that price would be impossible to find!" However, Jesus said, "...With men this is impossible, but with God all things are possible"

(Matthew 19:26, NKJV). Sure enough my car went to junk yard heaven not too long after that. In the meantime, I found out I was accepted to graduate school in Colorado and that they had a pretty good bus system throughout the city.

I didn't have time to focus on getting a car before I left, but I knew I was supposed to go to Colorado for school. I didn't need to worry about any more details than that. So I moved across the country without having a car. As mentioned previously, my friend Nicole took me to buy a bike. For four months, my transportation consisted of biking to school and occasionally riding the bus. This was a completely new, exciting and humbling experience for me.

As school was about to let out for the semester, I found out that the bus schedule for the city was going to be changed for the spring and would no longer be near my apartment. Everyone had warned me that the worst snows were in the spring time, especially March and that I probably won't be able to bike to school.

In the meantime, I got a call from my mom. Out of the blue, she tells me that my granddad wanted to give me his car. Yes, you heard me correctly. He wanted to give me his car. I was in a little bit of shock. To add to that, the car, although eight years old, only had 28,000 miles on it and it was a four-door. Additionally, the tag and insurance were much cheaper because it was an older model.

How amazing is that? And with ever so perfectly orchestrated timing that only God can arrange. "And my God shall supply all your needs according to His riches in glory by Christ Jesus" (Philippians 4:19, NKJV). I truly didn't need a car before January of that year. And with little ole' me from the south, experiencing my first winter in Colorado, I really had no idea what to expect. But God did.

What is also amazing to me is that I had prayed the "car prayer" two to three years before. I had completely forgotten that I had prayed that when I got the phone call from my mom. How amazing is it that although we may forget our requests, God never does. God knew my prayer for a car and provided for me in an even greater way than I had asked.

Kim

Enough Gas to make it home

When I was in high school, I witnessed the Lord answer my prayer request, right before my eyes. My friend, Misty, and I had gone Christmas shopping at the mall. We shopped until we dropped and spent every dime we had with us. Good thing we had a great day of shopping because much to our dismay when we returned to the car to leave the mall, we realized there was not enough gas in the car to make it home. As I just mentioned, we had no money to purchase gas either. This was before the days when every teenager in America had his or her own credit card and cell phone. In fact, I don't even think they had pay at the pump back then.

We started praying and searching in every nook and cranny of the car for spare money or change. We were in desperate need of divine intervention from the Lord. I remember praying and asking the Lord to allow us to make it home. Right before our very own eyes, I remember seeing the gauge for the gasoline move slightly away from empty. WHEW. PRAISE JESUS. We were going to make it home. Jesus gave us just the amount of gas that we needed to make it through our struggle that day.

I will never forget that encounter with Jesus as long as I live because I can remember specifically praying and seeing the Lord work immediately. Maybe in your own way you too can relate to my story. Perhaps you've had an encounter with Jesus that you know He alone met your very need right before your eyes. If you can't think of such a time, I encourage you to pray that He would open your eyes so that you may see Him. He is alive and active. He desires to meet us right where we are and answer our prayers. They may seem small and minuet in the big scheme of things, but with Jesus, nothing is too small to pray over. Praying for a little gas to make it home might seem so silly to some of you, buy hey, who knows? Had we not prayed, we just might have been stuck in the mall parking lot until this very day!

Heather

Housing

Colorado

I had just finished classes for graduate school and now had six months of internship ahead of me. For my internship, not only did I not get paid, but I had to pay tuition. I had to pay to work for free for six months. I also had to continue to pay for all my other expenses (housing, food, gas, etc.) My first internship, was forty hours a week and an hour commute down to Denver. Thus, I had to give up the part-time job I had while taking classes.

I thought, "There's no way I can do this unless I have a free place to live. I cannot afford to do my internship." Thus Heather and I prayed for me to have a free place to live that summer. My thoughts were initially that of being a caretaker for an elderly couple.

I was perusing through ads on the graduate bulletin board shortly thereafter. Sure enough, I came upon an ad for an elderly couple who needed someone to be there at night in case they needed anything. In return, free rent and utilities were provided. All I had to do was to spend the night. I knew as soon as I read it that this is where I'd be for the summer. I phoned the couple's daughter and then went to the house to meet the couple.

I would just like to tell you what an absolutely incredible place God provided for me that summer. God answered me in abundance. "Now to Him who is able to do exceedingly abundantly above all that we ask or think, according to the power that works in us" (Ephesians 3:20, NKJV). We prayed for a free place to live. Not only was it free, but it was magnificent. Imagine a Colorado summer in a home with the back porch facing the magnificent Rocky Mountains. What a breathtaking view to see every day. In addition, the home was very spacious. I got my own room, with two single beds in it (which was perfect since Heather came to visit me that summer.) I also had my own bathroom with a Jacuzzi tub in it. The neighborhood was on a golf course and there was a neighborhood pool. (I don't play golf, but I just thought I'd throw that tid bit in for free to give you an idea of the subdivision.) In addition, it was fifteen minutes closer for my commute to Denver. The home had air conditioning. Being from the south, I had no idea that most places out west did not have air conditioning. The university apartment where I had been living, was on the top floor of a three story building with no air conditioning. It was very small and stuffy. Thus, going to this home was a blessing in many ways and it was more reassurance that God answers specific prayers. He always takes care of the smallest details that we never even realized we were in need of. Great or small, God always meets our needs.

Kim

Scotland

I would like to give another example of trusting God with finances and where I lived. My second internship was in Scotland. I finished in Denver, packed up my car and drove across the country back to Georgia. I had about two days to unpack and repack for four months overseas. I did as much as I could on my part to find housing before I left. However, by the time I boarded the plane to head over, I had not found housing. Yet I was so confident in God's faithfulness that I didn't worry about it at all, but rather prayed about it. In fact, I was at times quite excited to tell people on the plane that I was moving to Scotland for the next few months and didn't know where I would live, but knew that God would provide something for me. And yes, a few times, people looked at me like I was crazy.

However, the flat that I ended up renting with friends was amazing. The price was reasonable and the location was beyond words. I lived in a flat off Rutland street in Edinburgh, the capital of Scotland. There was a castle around the corner. I got to walk by the castle every single day for the entire time I was there. For my British friends, I'm sure this isn't really a source of delight as you are quite accustomed to it. But for me, it was amazing. It was like being a part of a fairy tale. Here God was at work again. I seriously doubt that I would have found this flat on my own, without prayer and without God's intervention.

All I knew was that I was moving to Scotland, I had no place to live, I had prayed about it and I was trusting God. Again, I did not worry about the details. All I did was just show up and let God handle the rest. It truly is fun to have faith. Wait with anticipation and excitement over what God will do. Wait until you have a peace about something before making a decision. The longer you walk with the Lord, the more you will be able to have discernment regarding decisions.

It is almost beyond words to describe how magnificent it was to live by a castle. I felt like a little child at Christmas, unexpectedly surprised by a dream gift. It was truly the chance of a lifetime. And it was again God showing me, that He "is able to do *exceedingly* abundantly above all that we ask or think, according to the power that works in us" (Ephesians 3:20, NKJV).

Kim

Electricity Bill

If any of you have ever purchased a new home for the very first time at a young age, you can possibly relate to my next prayer story. I was only a year out of college, practically a brand new nurse. You know, brand new to having real money and the thoughts of real bills. After much prayer and consideration, I felt the Lord leading me to purchase my own home. I found the perfect town home and was soon a happy homeowner.

Purchasing a new home, of course, brings on new bills. I definitely had to form a budget and be very cautious with my money. I planned out all the bills that were due and knew exactly what all I needed to make it financially. Well, after receiving my very first electric bill, I went into a state of shock. (No pun intended!) It was in the $300 range. It blew me away. There was no way that a person living all by herself who worked night shift three nights a week and slept during the day could possibly use that much electricity. I had definitely not taken into consideration a bill that high when I planned my budget before purchasing my town home. What was I to do?

I sat for a day in the dark, with no lights on, no television or radio and barely any air conditioning thinking this was my only choice to not have a high bill next month. After a few hours of that, the shock factor ended and reality sunk in.

After the shock ended, I began to pray. Lord, you are in control of my finances and I know this will be a big learning situation for me. Please show me what I need to do to get this bill taken care of because I know it can't be correct.

I had the electric company come back and re-read the meter. Much to my dismay, it was read correctly. Okay, Lord, what is the next step? I had a person from the electric company come out to my house to see if there were any leaks anywhere or anything else that could have possibly gone wrong in my BRAND NEW town home to cause such a high bill. He found a problem with the wiring from the air conditioning unit. This led me to call the builder of the unit. That was no help. They were not willing to help me out at all and took no responsibility for the condition of the air conditioning unit.

I prayed again asking for the Lord's guidance and decided to call the company who installed the unit. Although the builder's were the responsible party and this company was not, they willingly took the responsibility. They were such a blessing from heaven. They were willing to come out to my home and fix the unit at no charge and also offered to pay for half of my electricity bill because the builders refused to help. Praise Jesus. The Lord knows our every need and takes care of His children.

Heather

Turkey dinner for Christmas

Not only have I over and over again witnessed the Lord answer the needs in my life but have also witnessed His hand upon the needs of others. I remember a time when a family at church was going through a rough time financially. It was only a few days until Christmas and they had no money and two sons to buy presents for. I remember them voicing their needs in choir practice one morning and confessing that they were simply going to trust the Lord to provide for their needs. As I already mentioned, they had no money for gifts or for Christmas dinner.

At the time, I worked for a local grocery store, Kroger, in the pharmacy. For Christmas that year, every employee received a free turkey and a $25 Kroger grocery gift card. Without a doubt, I knew exactly what I was supposed to do with the money and turkey. I felt compelled to give my gift to this family.

That night as my friend and I were leaving my home to deliver the gifts, my dad decided to contribute to their need by giving them money. I will forever hold in my heart the gratitude of this family. They were relying on the Lord and knew that He would meet their needs. Other forms of money came to them during that time period and I know it was all a work of the Lord and their trusting in Him to provide. It was a neat opportunity for the Lord to use me and my family in their time of need. It was also wonderful for me to witness first hand the Lord meeting the financial needs of that family.

Heather

Helping Others

Ever heard of the old adage, what goes around comes around? It applies to finances too. Finances, you say? Yes. "Well, I don't have any money to give to anyone," you may be thinking. Do you have an extra sweater? Do you have a loaf of bread? Do you have other tangible items that you can give someone else, no matter how small or insignificant they may seem? Have you ever volunteered your time at a homeless shelter? Maybe you sincerely do not have any money at all to give to anyone. However, you have the gift of time. You can give your time and your energies to encourage someone else.

We would like to ask you to ponder a few questions. Have you ever stopped to talk to or help the person on the side of the street holding the all too familiar sign "Please help, my family and I are starving." God's Word however, tells us, "Give to him who asks you, and from him who wants to borrow from you do not turn away" (Matthew 5:42 KJV.)

What if you do not take the time to help them? Then they go hungry another day. They go without warmth from the elements. They go with encouragement another day.

Below is my journal entry from November 2, 2004.

Today, I woke up early and I really felt that God was saying to me to work on the "Financial" section of this book. I thought, no problem, I can do that. I still have one of the old prayer boxes I made several years ago. I was going through it this morning and found a whole stack of index cards with financial verses I'd written on them years prior. As I started typing them out, I was reminded of the many times God has provided for me financially over the years.

I didn't finish this section because I had to go to work. But in the meantime, some of the verses were still on my mind. About mid-morning, my boss called me into her office. We sat down and she began to tell me that I got a fairly sizable raise. I was thinking, "praise the Lord." I was quite content with the salary that I had and was able to support myself. However, what more perfect day for me to find out about my increase?

During my drive home from work, I passed a man holding a sign. He was facing the other way. I think to myself, "I can't see what the sign says so I do not know if he is standing there because he is hungry." But I somehow *knew* that's what it said. God reminded me of the verses I'd typed this morning. "Whoever shuts his ears to the cry of the poor will also cry himself and not be heard" (Proverbs 21:13 NKJV). I was also reminded of the raise I'd just received. I turn around and went back, praying for the encounter I was about to have with this man. I drove by and was unable to hand him money or talk to him out of the window because of where he was standing in regards to oncoming traffic. I left the parking lot and turned around again. I knew God wanted me to go talk to him and not just drive by. So I drove back to him, parked the car and got out to talk to him.

As I got out of the car and was walking toward the man, another verse was going through my mind. "Don't forget to be kind to strangers, for some who have done this have entertained angels without realizing it." (Hebrews 13:2, TLB). As I approached, he called out to me to be careful because the area close to where he was standing was a little slick. Once I got up to him, I introduced myself to him, shook his hand and noticed what crystal clear blue eyes he had. I asked him to tell me about himself. He told me he was homeless and was worried about how cold it would be in the winter. We chatted for a few more minutes as he told me his story. I gave him some money and a power bar that I had in my purse. I don't usually carry any cash at all, but it just so happened that today I had a fairly decent amount of cash with me. I asked if there was anything I could pray for him about and he said just to pray over the story he'd just told me. I told him I would. He gave me a hearty smile and waved as I drove off.

God's word tells us to help the poor and those in need. It was and is not my place to judge this individual or any other based on the life circumstances that have caused them to be in such a place. It is my job to help people out in need. God gave me a raise today. The money is God's money. Not mine. Which again points us back to "Give to him who asks you, and from him who wants to borrow from you do not turn away" (Matthew 5:42, NKJV).

Kim

PRAYER

Father God,

I come before You and ask You to give me financial wisdom and direction. I thank You for all that You have blessed me with and given to me. I know that all that is here on earth belongs to You. Please teach me how to be a good steward of the money, time, talents and abilities that You have entrusted to me. I ask that You will guide my financial decisions.

Lord, I trust You and You alone to meet my every need. I ask You to provide me with food, clothing and shelter daily. I ask that when You show me how to be a good steward of what You've entrusted me with, that You will also show me how to use these to help others. I ask that You remind me of what You have blessed me with and help the love of money to never be a consuming factor in my life. I pray that You will teach me how to be a giving, generous person.

Lord, I also pray for the debts that I owe. I pray that You will help me to become debt-free. I pray that in so doing, I will be able to use the money You've entrusted me to, to help others and glorify you. In Acts 20:35 (NKJV), Paul tells us that he's "..shown (us) in every way, by laboring like this, that (we) must support the weak. And remember the words of the Lord Jesus, that He said, 'It is more blessed to give than to receive." Help me to remember this when I am making decisions regarding charges to my credit card, an extra home mortgage, a bigger home, a newer car and other materialistic possessions that are more for want than need.

Lord, I pray that You will remove the blinders from my eyes and help me not to be oblivious and ignorant to the cries of those in need. For I know, that one day, those could be my own cries. I pray that You guide my thought process with finances. As Romans 12:2 (NKJV) says, "And do not be conformed to this world, but be transformed by the renewing of your mind that you may prove what is that good and acceptable and perfect will of God."

In Jesus name,
Amen

VERSES

Philippians 4:19 (NKJV): "God shall supply all your needs according to His riches in glory by Christ Jesus."

Proverbs 22:7 (NKJV): ".....the borrower is servant to the lender."

Philippians 4:6 (NKJV): "Be anxious for nothing, but in everything by prayer and supplication, with thanksgiving, let your requests be made known to God."

Matthew 19:26 (NKJV): "..With men this is impossible, but with God all things are possible."

Philippians 4:19 (NKJV): "And my God shall supply all your needs according to His riches in glory by Christ Jesus."

Ephesians 3:20 (NKJV): "Now to Him who is able to do exceedingly abundantly above all that we ask or think, according to the power that works in us."

Matthew 5:42 (KJV): "Give to him who asks you, and from him who wants to borrow from you do not turn away."

Proverbs 21:13 (NKJV): "Whoever shuts his ears to the cry of the poor will also cry himself and not be heard."

Hebrews 13:2 (TLB): "Don't forget to be kind to strangers, for some who have done this have entertained angels without realizing it."

Acts 20:35 (NKJV): "I have shown you in every way, by laboring like this, that you must support the weak. And remember the words of the Lord Jesus, that He said, 'It is more blessed to give than receive."

Romans 12:2 (NKJV): "And do not be conformed to this world, but be transformed by the renewing of your mind that you may prove what is that good and acceptable and perfect will of God."

Psalm 37:16 (NKJV): "A little that a righteous man has is better than the riches of many wicked."

Psalm 41: 1 (NKJV): "Blessed is he who considers the poor; the Lord will deliver him in time of trouble."

Proverbs 11:24-25 (TLB): "It is possible to give away and become richer. It is also possible to hold on too tightly and lose everything. Yes, the liberal man shall be rich! By watering others, he waters himself."

Proverbs 14:21 (NKJV): "He who despises his neighbor sins; but he who has mercy on the poor, happy is he."

Proverbs 19:17 (NKJV): "He who has pity on the poor lends to the Lord, and He will pay back what he has given."

Proverbs 22:9 (NKJV): "He who has a generous eye will be blessed, for he gives of his bread to the poor."

Proverbs 22:16 (NKJV): "He who oppresses the poor to increase his riches, and he who gives to the rich, will surely come to poverty."

Proverbs 25:21 (NKJV): "If you enemy is hungry, give him bread to eat; and if he is thirsty, give him water to drink."

Proverbs 28:27 (NKJV): "He who gives to the poor will not lack, but he who hides his eyes will have many curses."

Proverbs 30:8-9 (TLB): "...Give me neither poverty nor riches! Give me just enough to satisfy my needs! For if I grow rich, I may become content without God. And if I am too poor, I may steal and thus insult God's holy name."

Ecclesiastes 11:1-2 (TLB): "Give generously, for your gifts will return to you later. Divide your gifts among many, for in the days ahead you yourself may need much help."

Matthew 23:23 (NKJV): "Woe to you, scribes & Pharisees, hypocrites! For you pay tithe of mint and anise and cummin, and have neglected the weightier matters of the law: justice and mercy and faith. These you ought to have done, without leaving the others undone."

Matthew 25:40 (NKJV): "And the King will answer and say to them, 'Assuredly, I say to you, inasmuch as you did it to one of the least of these My brethren, you did it to Me."

Ephesians 4:28 (NKJV): "Let him who stole steal no longer, but rather let him labor, working with his hands what is good, that he may have something to give him who has need."

1 Timonthy 6:10 (NKJV): "For the love of money is a root of all kinds of evil, for which some have strayed from the faith in their greediness, and pierced themselves through with many sorrows." (Notice this says "the *love* of money" not money itself. There is a big difference.)

CHAPTER NINE

SAFETY

We can not even begin to tell you how many times God has kept us safe. Countless times it seems. Thus the more He keeps us and those around us safe and protected, the more we pray for it.

A plane ride

God has kept me safe numerous times and in big ways. March 2002 I was flying from Denver back to Atlanta. I got nervous when I flew. I was a little more nervous on this particular flight because of the recent 9/11 attacks.

Heather prayed for me, as she always does when I fly. My flight ended up being delayed for a number of hours. It was delayed for so long that I missed my connecting flight in St. Louis. While I was in the Denver airport, I met some really nice girls from Montana. Since we were all stuck in the airport together, we sat together and talked. Not really much else to do and even if I did get upset about the delay, it wouldn't have solved anything.

Once we were finally able to board, I overheard a flight attendant tell the passengers behind me that the flight was delayed because of suspicious activity for which the FBI had been called. He told them he could not go into more detail than this. However, they had to switch planes because of it.

Finally when I made it to St. Louis, I found that there were no more flights to Atlanta that evening. So not only did I miss the connecting flight, but I couldn't get re-booked on another flight until the morning. The airline's headquarters was having problems with the tracking system. Due to this, it wasn't safe for any of their planes to be in the air as they would be unable to track and monitor them. Hundreds of passengers were grounded until the morning.

The next morning I was able to get a fairly early flight to Atlanta. There was a nice gentleman sitting next to me. Come to find out he was in the worship band at his church in Pennsylvania. We had a very uplifting, inspiring conversation.

Once I arrived in Atlanta, I began thinking back to Heather's prayer for me. And it gave me goose bumps. She had specifically prayed three things for me: for there not to be any terrorist activity on the plane, for no instrument failure and for me to have an uplifting conversation with the person beside me. I started thinking - What if she'd never prayed those things for me? What if they hadn't caught the terrorist activity before switching planes? What if I'd been on the plane when the problems with headquarters began? What if...??

"For I am persuaded that neither death, nor life, nor angles nor principalities nor powers, nor things present nor things to come, nor *height* nor depth, nor any other created thing, shall be able to separate us from the love of God which is in Christ Jesus our Lord" (Romans 8:38-39, NKJV).

Kim

The Boulder in Denver

Here's my journal entry from August 17, 2003:

I was driving home from Denver to Ft Collins after a blind date last night at 1:30 AM. I was sleepy and nodding off, so I prayed for safety getting home and for the Lord to keep me awake. Right as I finished, something told me to look at these guys standing on a bridge I was about to cross under. "Don't take your eyes of the guy on the bridge. Don't take your eyes off the guy. Don't take your eyes off." These thoughts kept going through my mind. My first thought was that one was going to jump. There were two cars on the bridge and one guy had a huge boulder or something of the sort in his hands. As I approached, I noticed he was raising it above his head. As I was about to go under the bridge he threw it over at me. Had I not been watching, it would have hit my windshield directly. I swerved to miss it and fish tailed for a bit. My heart was pounding. I certainly was wide awake with all the adrenaline going through me. But praise the Lord there were no other cars near me or I would have hit them. Praise the Lord I prayed and He protected me from harm. What would have happened had I not prayed? What would've happened had I not listened to the answer?

Kim

Labor Day 2004, San Destin, Florida

I was in a prayer group during a singles retreat with North Point Community Church. We went around in a circle and prayed for the person on our left. My friend, Tony, was sitting beside me. He prayed for me to have a safe trip home and for me to be an encouragement to someone along the way. Not too long afterwards, the retreat was over and I headed back to Atlanta.

My friend, Brita and I headed back around six pm Sunday evening. On the way home, I kept thinking that I needed to be sure to stop somewhere, maybe a gas station, so I could be an encouragement to someone. About half way home just before we crossed into Georgia, I suggested we stop. Our stop was no longer than five minutes, but I spent the whole time diligently looking around to find whoever it may be that God wanted me to be an encouragement to. However, there really wasn't anyone there. We got back in the car and I thought to myself, "Well, I tried."

Within a minute of getting back on the interstate, a police car flew past us with his lights flashing. We came up on the scene of a horrible accident that had just happened only moments before. The smell of the accident was very intense before we even saw what happened. The smoke from the accident was still a good twenty feet above the overpass. It involved two semi-trucks on both sides of the interstate and a number of cars behind them that had either piled up or ran off the road because of the accident. One semi was still on fire. There were people standing along the interstate still looking a bit dazed.

We drove along in silence for a few moments because the scene was so horrible. I don't know if any of the people involved were from our singles retreat or not. After we got a little further down the road, Brita reached over and patted me on the back. She said, "you know, if you wouldn't have needed to stop at the gas station, we would have been in that accident." We were also in a convertible, which could have proven catastrophic for us.

The ONLY reason I suggested we stop was because of Tony's prayers from our group that morning. Who knows if anyone else would've prayed those exact words? Who knows if I would've stopped for any other reason than for what was prayed that morning? Sometimes God delays us for a reason. Instead of becoming angry or frustrated, we must always be thankful. He may be delaying our steps in order to keep us from harm.

Kim

Protecting our Home

Have you ever lived in fear? You know, the fear that grips you and keeps you from sleeping soundly at night. Through the next story, I learned to have faith in the Lord and allow Him to replace my fears with Himself.

My husband and I were so excited the day we bought our very first house. It was a warm and cozy, quaint yellow ranch. The perfect house for us at the time. The neighborhood was just as quaint and very quiet.

Two years after we moved there, we started hearing rumors of minor thefts in the neighborhood. Not too long after, we started hearing of burglaries in several of the homes as well as cars driving through the neighborhood that didn't belong. These mishaps began concerning my husband and I. This terrified me and led me to want to move from my neighborhood.

We didn't feel it was the Lord's will for us to move at that time. Instead of placing a "For Sale" sign in the front yard, we decided to pray in our yard. I am not talking about a little part of our yard. We prayed over all of it. We circled around our entire property line. I am sure that our neighbors thought we were parading around the house. We weren't actually parading, but praying. During this prayer that covered our entire property line, we asked the Lord to protect our family, our house and for Him to keep us safe. We asked Him to turn our fears into faith. He did just that. We were no longer afraid because we trusted that the Lord would keep us safe and protected. And He did.

We have since moved from that home, but for the remainder of our time there, we had no burglaries, thefts and most importantly.....NO FEAR! 1 Peter 5:7 (NIV), "Cast all your anxiety on Him because He cares for you."

Heather

Such a sense of humor...

Who ever said that God didn't have a sense of humor? Read on, because God does have a sense of humor.

I've certainly kept up with having Heather praying for me every single time I fly. So much so that now it's almost comical. Thus, I thought I'd share with you another flying escapade. I was flying from Atlanta to Denver in January 2005 to attend a wedding ceremony in Breckenridge for my friends, Lauren and Jeremy. Of course, I had Heather pray before take off.

As I was sitting in my seat, chilled out and relaxed, we began to experience turbulence. But I thought, no worries the plane trip was covered in prayer. Then the pilot came on to say the following, "Ladies and gentlemen, I would like to inform you that the bumpiness you are experiencing is not turbulence, but it is in fact, the aircraft itself. However, the mechanic in Atlanta has assured me that everything is fine and thus we are going to press on to Denver."

After the pilot's announcement and my momentary adrenaline rush, I sat there and remembered Heather's prayer. Her prayer this time was, "God, please don't let there be any mechanical trouble." I was confident we were going to be fine. Sure enough, we landed safely a short time later.

Kim

PRAYER

Lord,

I come before You and ask for You to protect me from harm. I ask that You protect me physically, emotionally, mentally and spiritually. I ask that You protect me from Satan's attacks and keep me safe. I pray that You will let me know when a situation or person is unsafe for me to be around. I pray that You will guide my footsteps and keep me from harm.

I pray that You will protect my family and friends from harm and danger. I pray that You put a hedge of protection around me when I travel, drive to and from work and sleep at night. I pray that You will guard my home and protect me from intruders. I pray that You are my shield as I trust in You.

In Jesus name,
Amen

VERSES

Romans 8:38-39 (NKJV): "For I am persuaded that neither death, nor life, nor angles nor principalities nor powers, nor things present nor things to come, nor *height* nor depth, nor any other created thing, shall be able to separate us from the love of God which is in Christ Jesus our Lord."

1 Peter 5:7 (NIV), "Cast all your anxiety on Him because He cares for you."

Psalm 3:3 (NKJV): "But You, O Lord, are a shield for me, my glory and the One who lifts up my head."

Psalm 5:12 (NIV): "For surely, O Lord, you bless the righteous; you surround them with Your favor as with a shield."

Psalm 18:30b (NKJV): "...He is a shield to all who trust in Him."

Psalm 18:48 (NKJV): "He delivers me from my enemies. You also lift me up above those who rise against me; You have delivered me from the violent man."

Psalm 28:7 (NKJV): "The Lord is my strength and my shield; my heart trusted in Him and I am helped; therefore my heart greatly rejoices, and with my song I will praise Him."

Habakkuk 3:19 (TLB): "The Lord God is my strength; he will give me the speed of a deer and bring me safely over the mountains."

Eph 6:16 (NKJV): "Above all, taking the shield of faith with which you will be able to quench all the fiery darts of the wicked one."

CHAPTER TEN

11:59

One of my favorite verses in the entire Bible is Psalm 37:4 (NIV). It reads as follows, "Delight yourself in the Lord and He will give you the desires of your heart." Sounds like a good verse, huh?

I would love to share with you why this verse has impacted my life in such a way. I would like to give you the "Heather" interpretation of this verse. First, however, let me tell you what I think this verse does not mean. I think many people misinterpret this verse. Some may think that as long as we seek or "delight" in the Lord, then we should be able to have anything we ask for. Wrong. I do not feel that is the way the Lord intended for this verse to be interpreted. He did not mean for us to say we follow Him, then ask for a brand new car, a brand new spouse, a million dollars, etc. and the "poof" there is our request. That may have happened on the television series, "I Dream of Jeannie," but that is not how the Lord works.

Let's dive into this verse and see all it has to offer. It has a great deal to offer. I believe that the Lord calls us to worship Him. He is calling each of us to a deeper longing for Himself. He yearns for us to seek up and His awesome plan for every aspect of our lives. If you are truly following

Christ and seeking His will for every aspect of your life, then you will have the desires of your heart. This is because your desires will be in alignment with the very desires that He has already prepared for you in advance. All we have to do is get on the same page that He is on for our lives and get excited for what the plan entails. His desires will become our desires and we can ask for them because they are already mapped out for us according to the Lord's will for our lives.

I really want you to grasp the point I am trying to get across to you. When I have my daily prayer time with the Lord, I come before Him and ask Him to align my desires up with the desires that He has already prepared for me in advance. I believe that the Lord does exactly this. Eventually, I feel that as I pray and pray over a matter, my prayers become what He already desires for me because I have asked Him to place these very things on my heart as well as rid me of the desires that are not of Him. Therefore, more times than not, I feel that the things I am asking of the Lord are given to me because He already had them planned for me before I even knew them to be a desire of my very own. Prayer is taken to a deeper level when our desires are in alignment with the Lord's very desires for our lives.

My husband and I decided not to find out the sex of our third child. We did this for our firstborn and really preferred to be surprised at birth. Everyone thought we were absolutely crazy because we already had two boys. We didn't mind the unknown, even if the baby ended up being another son. We knew the Lord had a perfect plan for our family and the sex was up to Him and nobody else.

I secretly desired a baby girl, but would have been absolutely thrilled to be the mother of three boys. As I prayed over this little baby that was growing in my womb, I felt the Lord impress upon my heart that exact verse Psalm 37:4. This verse would come to mind every single time I prayed. Claiming this verse led me to believe that I was going to have a baby girl. I know many mothers say that you "just know" the sex of your baby. I never had that "mother's tuition" with my two sons but really felt that my third child was going to be a girl because of the scripture the Lord impressed upon my heart. The only person I told this revelation to was my husband.

My deep desire was to have a baby girl and on September 29, 2008 as I delighted in Him, he allowed that desire to become a reality. I am the blessed mother of a precious baby girl, Emma Rose.

Sharing my feelings on Psalm 37:4 with you is a very good opener for our next section of prayers. We like to refer to this section as 11:59, otherwise known as God's perfect timing. God is righteous and just, as is His timing. He is an "on time" God. We may begin to doubt that from time to time but He hasn't failed us yet. He always proves Himself true and we must believe that He timing is always right. One thing we've consistently noticed over our years of praying together, is that if you need something by 12:00, you will get it at 11:59.

We encourage you as you read over our next section to open your hearts to what God is leading you to pray. Seek Him sincerely. Dig deep and pray BIG! We pray that you will be encouraged as you read about how we have trusted an on-time God and His perfect 11:59 timing. As you have read over and over again, we both believe that we serve an on time God.

Do you trust Him and His perfect timing? Are you willing to "go out on a limb" and trust Him to do the impossible? Are you eager to see Him work in and through your prayer requests in ways that are almost impossible for the human eye to believe? We pray that the following glimpses of our hearts will inspire you in such a way. Make a list and see what the Lord desires to do with your requests. Start small and pray big.

Roommates

Why worry about things before you need them? One reason you may worry about an outcome is because of lack of faith or trust in God. All you need to do is pray about it, do what you can from a human perspective and trust God with His word. Philippians 4:6-7 NKJV, "Be anxious for nothing, but in everything by prayer and supplication, with thanksgiving, let your requests be made known to God, and the peace of God, which surpasses all understanding, will guard your hearts and minds through Christ Jesus."

I made my first list of "impossible" things to pray for when I was in college. Matthew 19:26 NKJV, "With man this is impossible, but with God all things are possible." After transferring to the University of Georgia to complete my undergrad degree, I began to pray for the following year.

One of my closest friends, Becki, and I were roommates at the time. We decided we wanted to have more roommates the next year, in order to meet more people. I prayed that by June 1, Becki and I would know where to live for the next year and for us to know who our roommates would be. I prayed for nearly six months for June 1, 1996.

On May 31, neither of us had any idea where we'd be living or who we'd be living with. Yet, I had complete peace about it and was rather looking forward to what God was going to do the next day. We weren't under a deadline or pressure to make a decision by June 1. I just picked that day as part of my prayer. I happened to run into my good friend John that night by coincidence and he told me about some new apartments where he and his friends were going to be living. He recommended that I check them out.

June 1, 1996 Becki and I went to look at the apartments and we signed a lease for a larger apartment, as a leap of faith, that we'd have more roommates. I *knew* without a doubt that we were doing the right thing and I *knew* that we'd find at least one other roommate that very day. The reason I knew this was because it was June 1, the day that I had prayed for.

We returned home and within an hour or so received a call from a girl who stated she knew we were looking for a roommate and wanted to know if there was still something available. Without a doubt, I knew this was the person who was to live with us.

I spent so much time in prayer for roommates because I knew we'd be living with complete strangers for an entire year and I wanted to live with whoever God planned. Without a doubt, this was my most memorable year in college. I met so many wonderful people that year.

I am so thankful I held out until the very last minute. Had I taken anything else or any other roommate offers a moment sooner, it would not have been nearly as perfect. It was not sheer coincidence that all of these details unfolded in such a way. Since then, I've been able to trust God in situations that require a much bigger leap of faith.

This was one of the first times I truly experienced God answering a prayer by a certain date. It solidified my faith. No one knew I was praying this and no one knew I had picked out that date. It was amazing to me. This was *only* between me and God. The God of the universe cared enough about a college student requesting roommates that He answered me on the day I asked for. Not a moment sooner.

Kim

Music City Bound

To best explain the next answer to prayer and God's 11:59 timing, I am more than eager to be transparent with you and actually give you a revised email that I sent to many people. I sent this after praying and allowing the Lord to relocate me from Atlanta, Georgia to Nashville, Tennessee.

August 19, 2002

I pray this email finds you all having a lovely day!

I am writing ya'll because I am just bursting inside to share with each of you the awesome things that the Lord has done in my life in the past several weeks and to also send a note of thanks to each of you.

As most of you know, I have been praying for some time now about moving to Nashville. In order for me to move, several things had to happen. God is so good. I have learned that if He wants you somewhere, He will certainly change the impossible to possible. He has strengthened my trust and stretched my faith in Him. A main verse that He used in my life is Matthew 17:20 (NIV) "...if you have faith as small as a mustard seed....nothing will be impossible for you."

We serve an on time God. He has proven that to me over and over again these past few months. I want to share with each of you just how He did that.

The Lord started laying on my heart last October the desire to move to Nashville. Only one person knew this (my prayer partner, Kim).

In December, my dear friend, Tammy, a med student at the time, had an interview at Vanderbilt in Nashville, for her residency. She knew my love for Nashville and asked if I wanted to come along for her interview. She ended up loving the interview and the program. We joked that if she ended up living in Nashville that I would move there as well. Neither of us ever imagined that I would really end up there. In the meantime Kim and I prayed about Nashville off and on.

In March, Tammy got accepted to the residency program at Vanderbilt. At that point, it was still somewhat of a joke that I would move there too.

For two and a half months, Kim and I fervently prayed for specifics and discernment. We felt the only way we would for sure know if my relocation was the Lord's desire and not my own, was for my townhouse to sell or be rented.

Well....for several more months nothing happened. It was as if the Lord gave me a peace about moving to Nashville and then became silent. No jobs opened up and no bites on my house at all. I sought the Lord in prayer. He taught me so much through the silence. I even got to the point that all I could do one night was to get on my knees before Him and cry out to Him, that I wasn't even sure I had any more faith to give Him. This is where the above verse in Matthew comes in. I was reminded of the mustard seed verse several times that same weekend. That Sunday, I fell before the Lord and told Him that I hoped my mustard seed faith was enough because that was all I had to offer. All I had to give Him was faith the size of a mustard seed, which isn't all that big. I knew that if He wanted me in Nashville then He would sell or rent my house and would get me there...but WHEN???

I decided to ask the Lord to sell/rent out my house by August 1. I thank each of you from the bottom of my heart who prayed for and with me.

On July 31, a woman called my house after reading the ad in the paper and wanted to come by that day to take a look at the house. My friend Shannon called me that afternoon to remind me that the next day was August 1. Therefore, God was going to work that day. I hadn't even realized that August 1 was the very next day. Oh my! God had to work today!

Well...that evening, the woman came by and was excited to rent my townhouse for a year. Praise Jesus. We serve an on time God! I was excited and blessed beyond imagination. But oh no! The only weekend that I had in the near future to move, outside of taking days off of work, would be that very weekend. I had better round up folks to help me move since I couldn't afford to hire movers.

Please continue to read...I know this is a long story...but God stories are continuing to happen. Just read on and you will be amazed.

I made phone calls to just about every guy that I could think of and not a soul was going to be able to help me move that weekend for various reasons. The Lord reminded me that I need not worry because I had already given Him all the faith I had. He would work out every detail and I had to trust Him.

Tammy called to tell me that a friend from college, Charles, was going to be in town for a few weeks and offered to help. Graciously Charles helped..but..where would I find someone else to help? Well..our on time God led Kim and I to Lowe's to visit her friend John. This was two hours before Charles was to come help me move. John offered to come and help Charles move all he could during his one hour dinner break. They were awesome and worked so hard. A lot was loaded into the Ryder truck that hour but there was still a few heavy things left after John had to return to work. Upon returning home after a bite to eat, my neighbor insisted on helping Charles move the rest of the heavy objects. He must have been dropped straight from heaven. What a blessing. They moved the rest of the heavy objects. Thank you so much Charles, John and Dana. Also thank you Kim for your very big Popeye muscles that you used while helping me move.

My parents, Kim and I made the drive to Nashville on Saturday morning and were worry free, or so I thought.

Tammy and Kim helped unload the small stuff and all we had left were the big things for Tammy's guy friends to unload the next day. Well...as if my faith hadn't been stretched already, God decided that it needed a little more stretching. One of Tammy's friends was not able to help us unload, leaving us with only one guy and knowing not a soul in Nashville that could help. This happened around six pm on Sunday. You know, just before dark, the night the truck had to be returned.

Well..no fear. God is near. Kim had the bright idea to go back to the church that we attended that morning and seek help. What an awesome idea. The college and career leader rounded up six or seven guys to come over and help. They knocked out the heavy stuff in about twenty minutes. Thank you Christ Church guys, Jeannie, Bob, Kim and Tammy. We serve an on time God.

Thank you all for taking the time to read what the Lord did for me. He is so awesome! He has taught me so much through this. My cup runneth over. I would not have survived all this without your prayers and encouraging words. Thank you for each prayer lifted to heaven, thank you for each encouraging card, email and verse. Thank you for each box you lifted. I thank you for everything you did. I am forever grateful.

I am music city bound! Nope, not to get a singing career in country music. I still plan on being a nurse, working in pediatrics. I will be permanently in Nashville as of September 13.

May the Lord bless each of you for all you have done for me.

Love in Christ,

Heather

October 2002

Have you ever had one of those moments when something amazing happens and all you can think in that moment, is that was a "God thing?" Do you know what I mean? You know it when it happens and it usually doesn't have to hit you over the head like a load of bricks. You are very aware of it as a "God thing." Well, that "God thing" just happened to me as I began to write about my next amazing answered prayer.

I was looking up a verse for another section and in my Bible I came across Matthew 17:14-21 instead. I was using my old, rusty, pages half torn out, words written all in the margins so that you can barely read the scriptures, Bible. I love that Bible. It is full sermon notes, words inspired to me by the Lord as I have spent time in the Word and many, many prayers and dates of answered prayers.

In the margin of those verses I had two separate prayer requests written. One was from July 2002 when I was praying for the Lord to sell or rent my townhouse in order for me to be able to move to Nashville, Tennessee (as you just read in a previous story). How awesome was it to look back upon those verses and see how the Lord has brought me so far from that prayer request. Just beside that prayer I also had a request dated October 2002. God is so good.

I was about to sit down to write about how the Lord answered my prayer for a husband. He knew that I was to write on that topic next. He led me to the very section in my Bible that I prayed over as I desired and asked the Lord to send my husband into my life. October 2002 was the month that I earnestly prayed for the Lord to allow me to meet my future husband. And guess what? I did. What a "God thing." I hope you are as excited as I am about "God things" because they are so amazing. He never ceases to amaze me when He over and over again reveals Himself to me.

Let me begin with saying this: I do not always just ask the Lord for something randomly just for the sake of asking. For the most part, when I truly seek the Lord and ask for a specific prayer it is usually because He first stirred my heart and led me to pray for a specific request. As I mentioned more than once in this book, I always claim Psalm 37:4. I so strongly agree with this verse and how the Lord speaks to me through it, that I want to share it with you again. Psalm 37:4, NIV states that you are to "delight yourself in the Lord and He will give you the desires of your heart." To me that verse does not mean to ask the Lord for anything you want and you shall receive it. I feel that verse is telling us that if we are truly delighting in the Lord and earnestly seeking Him then the things that we desire, we can ask for. This is because, more than likely, they are already desires that He has inspired within our hearts. I truly claim that verse when I feel the Lord stirring my heart to pray over a specific request.

In October 2002 I felt the Lord stirring my heart and leading me to use that month to earnestly seek Him in the area of desiring to have a husband. About a year and a half prior to the month of October I wanted a husband so badly that it almost consumed my thoughts. I didn't like feeling that way, so I began to pray for the Lord to take those consuming thoughts away from me. He did. Months passed as I was enjoying my time as a single woman and the thoughts of marriage no longer consumed me. After some time I felt the Lord stir within my heart the desire to have a husband once again. However, this time it wasn't like before when the thoughts consumed me. I felt the Lord leading me to specifically pray that He would bring the man that I was to marry into my life in the month of October. I had no idea why at that time and how that would happen. I had just moved to Nashville the month prior and at that point only knew a few people, none of whom were male. Only a few people knew I was praying for this to happen and I asked them to pray this prayer along with me. I asked them to pray that the Lord would allow the man I was to marry to come into my life in the month of October. As I just mentioned I had moved to Nashville and was in search of a job. My initial job offer fell through. I applied at several hospitals as well as with the health department, seeking a job as a pediatric nurse. Several weeks later, I was offered a position as a school nurse at a local high school. I willingly accepted the job offer because I had no other options at the time. In the meantime the days of October were passing me by. I continued to pray for my husband but I saw no fruit to my prayers. Thank the Lord that He laid it upon my heart to pray to meet my husband during a month that had thirty-one days.

The first day at the high school was at the end of October. I had a horrible first day at the new school and there was no "future husband" in my sight as far as I knew. On the very last day of October, my friend Jeannie invited me and my roommate, Tammy to a get together one of her friends was having. Hhmm, Christians gathering, that must be it! My future husband has got to be at the get together. Count me in! Well, the last day of October came and went, along with the get together and you guessed it... no future husband in sight.

Okay, I am sure you are just as confused as I was at that moment in my life. Here it was November first and I had no idea why the Lord impressed upon my heart for me to pray for the man I was to marry to come into my life during the month of October. Listen once again to the prayer that I prayed for the month of October.

Lord, I pray that you bring into my life the man that I am supposed to spend the rest of my life with during the month of October.

Notice the words "bring into my life." I never prayed that I would actually *meet* him, that he would ask me out or that I would know him personally that month. I only prayed for him to come into my life. Guess what? He did. Praise Jesus. Glory to God in the highest. Friends, I am writing this section to you as a married woman.

A few weeks into November, there was a rumor around the front office at the high school that I had a secret admirer. A week or so after this rumor was heard, a coworker asked if I would be willing to meet this mystery man. He had noticed me the first day or so of my job there as the school nurse. Yes, it was at the very end of October. It just took him a few weeks to approach me. Willingly, I told the coworker that I would meet him and little did I know that behind my clinic door stood my future husband. The Lord was working in my life in October and my future husband did come into my life that same month.

As with most instances in my life if it is prayed over to occur at 12:00 it is going to become a reality at 11:59. Again, this can be referred to as God's "11:59 timing." I say it somewhat jokingly. However, it is so very true for my life. The very last day of October was the first day at my new job and the very place that my future husband would come into my life. We met and began dating. As you may have heard people say before, it was as if we had known each other our entire lives. It was very different than any other feeling I have had with previous guys I dated. There was such a sense of peace. I could truly claim the promise of God in 1 Corinthians 14:33, NIV, that God is not a God of disorder but a God of peace. A year later from our very first date we were married "happily ever after." Now seven years and three children later, we are still happily married and blessed. God is good. God is good. Say that out loud with me. "God is good."

Now, unless you totally feel the leading of the Lord, don't put this book down this very second and put a hole in your jeans by kneeling and praying for the Lord to send your future spouse this very month. I didn't pray lightly for God to do such a thing. The Lord took me through a long process before I felt Him leading me to pray for my future husband to come into my life during the month of October. However, I do encourage you, if you are not already in the habit of doing so, to begin to pray for your future spouse. Kim and I have been praying for many years now for the Lord to prepare us and our future spouses for one another. I truly feel that until we and our spouses are ready that it will not be the marriage that the Lord intends for us. Boyfriends and dates before Jeff even entered my life I was praying for him without even knowing his name. The Lord was preparing both of us for the right time. Until we were both ready, the timing was never right. Believe me, I did not then nor ever want to get in front of God's perfect timing.

Don't give up praying and believing, my friend. If it is truly a desire of your heart and the will of the Lord for you to marry, you will. It may not be on your timetable but the Lord's. It may be hard to believe it right now, but He does have the man or woman He desires for you to spend happily ever after with waiting for you. He is just waiting on the perfect time for both of you. Keep praying and in the meantime don't let the desire consume you. I loved being single and enjoyed all it had to offer. Even now I look back on the time that I had as a single woman and smile because it was such a neat time in my life. There was a freedom tied to singleness like no other. I am very thankful for that time in my life. If you are single, you can use this time for God's glory. My prayers are with you, my friend as you wait for God's best.

Heather

Cinco de Mayo

In August of 2005 my husband and I found out some very wonderful news. We were expecting a baby! Our expected due date was May the second. What joyful news we were able to share with our family and friends. We realized that it would be really neat if I gave birth a few days late and his or her birthday was on May 5, 2005. How neat to be able to say 05-05-05 for a birth date. My husband and I decided to pray for that to be our delivery date. Of course it wasn't on the top of our list and yes it was a very silly, small prayer request but we decided to pray for that day. The Lord tells us to come to Him about anything. Besides, He already knows our hearts before we ask Him so why not verbalize what was on our heart. We really didn't pray over it daily but just thought it would be a neat birthday for our child to have.

I had a wonderful, uneventful pregnancy but by the end I was ready to have my baby. May 2 came and no baby. We heard and tried every old wives tale possible to induce labor, from eating spicy food to driving over the railroad tracks. Jeff's dad told us we couldn't just drive any vehicle over the railroad tracks, it had to be a truck. So we got in our big green truck and drove over the railroad tracks. Another evening my husband came home from work and told me that we needed to jump on the bed to help induce labor. So up on the bed we climbed and jumped like we were little kids. The days came and went and no baby.

What were we thinking trying to have this baby before May 5? That is what we prayed and that is exactly what the Lord had in store. After several nights of minimal contractions my doctor decided to induce labor. Guess what the day was? May 5! It was a very long day of labor. Finally at 10 pm the nurse said it was time for me to begin the delivery process. I remember telling her that she had two hours to get my baby out because I prayed for 5-5-05. She told me that it was up to me if I had the baby before midnight. Well, it was up to God and His perfect timing. No, I didn't have our precious little Jonah at 11:59 that night but it was close. I had him at 11:16 p.m. Wow! We serve an on time God. I think He is very humorous and I am surprised that He didn't have me wait to deliver until 11:59. Nonetheless, my son's birthday is 05-05-05! What a fun birthday. Not only is it a cool date to remember but it was also the National Day of Prayer and Cinco de Mayo. God is good.

Many people knew that we were praying for that date to deliver our son. I know it is a very small and minute request but what a testimony to those who knew we were asking the Lord for it. I know it impacted the prayer lives of a few distinct people. I pray that our prayer for that day was a testimony of the power of God.

It is such a wonderful joy to be a mommy. We have since had two other children and God has allowed me and my husband to experience a love for them we never imagined. It is just a taste of the amount of love our Heavenly Father has for us. What an honor to be able to pray over our children and watch as they grow up the Lord. Praise Jesus for answering prayer and praise Jesus for being an ON TIME God.

I John 3:1a (NIV): "How great is the love the Father has lavished on us, that we should be called children of God..."

Heather

PRAYER

Oh Father, we come to You at this time and pray that You strengthen our prayer lives. Call us to pray. May we get on track with Your perfect timing. May we be challenged and strengthened.

May You hear our heart cries and answer our calls to You, our on time God. Oh, Jesus, may we fall before your face and seek You. Oh Lord, if there is a sister or brother in need of You, reach out to them and hear them. If someone is at the edge of a cliff (whatever their cliff may be) and not sure whether to jump or stay on board, may You speak to them. Reveal Yourself to them in such a way that there is no mistaking it for anyone other than You. Use the faith they have even if it is only the size of a mustard seed. Thank You in advance, Oh Father, for what you are about to do in our lives as we are called to pray and believe! Father God, help me to realize that You always have perfect timing in our life events. You created me for a reason and a purpose. Help me not to get so caught up in the details of life that they cause me stress. Help me to remember and know that You are the one guiding my footsteps and my life plan.

Lord, I pray that You will help us "be anxious for nothing, but in everything by prayer and supplication, let (my) requests be made known to (You)" so that Your peace, "which surpasses all understanding, will guard (my) heart and mind through Christ Jesus" (Philippians 4:6-7).

I pray Lord that You will remind us to trust you through all my life circumstances. Help us to trust You and not be anxious when we do not know how things will work out. Help us to know that You handle even the smallest detail of our lives with perfect timing.

In Jesus name,

AMEN!

VERSES

Psalm 37:4 (NIV): "Delight yourself in the Lord and He will give you the desires of your heart."

Matthew 19:26 (NKJV): "With man this is impossible, but with God all things are possible."

Matthew 17:20 (NIV): "He replied, "Because you have so little faith. I tell you the truth, if you have faith as small as a mustard seed, you can say to this mountain, 'Move from here to there' and it will move. Nothing will be impossible for you"

1 Corinthians 14:33 (NIV): "God is not a God of disorder but a God of peace."

Philippians 4:6-7 (NKJV): "Be anxious for nothing, but in everything by prayer and supplication, with thanksgiving, let your requests be made known to God, and the peace of God, which surpasses all understanding, will guard your hearts and minds through Christ Jesus."

Matthew 21:22 (NKJV): "And whatever you ask in prayer, believing, you will receive."

I John 3:1a (NIV): "How great is the love the Father has lavished on us, that we should be called children of God..."

Notes

Forward
1. Matilda Erickson Andross, *Alone with God: fitting for service*, (Mountain View, California: Pacific Press Publishing Association, 1917), p. 128

Chapter 7
1. Corrie Ten Boom, *The Hiding Place* (Peabody, Massachusetts: Hendrickson Publishers, 2006), p. x